Speak
for
Yourself

About the Author

Cristina Stuart is Britain's foremost trainer of speaking skills. She is the founder of Speak First, a highly regarded training organisation which has enabled thousands of professionals to overcome their fear of talking in public and giving presentations. She has taught personnel from many of the UK's leading companies as well as coached individuals, politicians and other public figures.

Cristina is a founder member of the Professional Speakers' Association, a member of the Institute of Public Relations, a fellow of the Royal Society for the encouragement of Arts, Manufactures and Commerce (RSA) and a certified NLP practitioner.

Cristina Stuart

Speak for Yourself

Revised Edition

How to give persuasive presentations and entertaining talks – with confidence

PIATKUS

For my brother John whose curiosity and energy
were an inspiration for all who knew him

First published in 2000 by
Piatkus Books Ltd
5 Windmill Street
London W1T 2JA
e-mail: info@piatkus.co.uk

Reprinted 2001

This revised edition published 2005

The moral rights of the author have been asserted

A catalogue record for this book is available from the British Library

ISBN 0 7499 2593 0

Text design by Paul Saunders
Edited by Carol Franklin and Krystyna Mayer

Typeset by Action Publishing Technology Ltd, Gloucester
Printed and bound in Great Britain by
Mackays Ltd, Chatham, Kent

Contents

PART THREE – **Practicalities**

Acknowledgements

There are a number of people who have contributed to this book in both a direct and an indirect way. Over the years the Speak First trainers have evolved and developed my original ideas and I would like especially to thank Clare Willis for her unflagging energy, Caroline Limpus for her contribution to the chapter on voice, Rudi Szczerba for his comments on the visual aids chapters, Neil McNeil for the chapter on dealing with the media and Isobel Jensen and Patrick Burke for their significant contribution over many years. Susie Kershaw's help was invaluable for the chapter on multi-cultural audiences.

Finally, I would like to acknowledge my editors, Vicky Wilson and Gill Bailey, for their encouragement and guidance during the writing of this.

Introduction

If you have taken this book down from the bookshop shelf it's probably because you have a need to speak with more confidence in certain situations. If you were attracted by the book title then you will certainly learn a lot from the contents. I will take you through some easy-to-follow guidelines that will enable you to understand and practise how to successfully put across your ideas in a variety of different settings.

You may have concerns about speaking in public and you are not alone. This is a very common fear and in some ways I have benefited from that fear for twenty years: I have taught thousands of nervous speakers how to cope with their anxiety and have opened up for them the possibility of actually enjoying public speaking. That might seem a long way off for you right now – however, this book will show you how to express yourself with more assurance. With time, who knows, you might even find it pleasurable.

This is the second edition of the book and I have broadened the original version to include a number of social and semi-social situations, from giving a formal speech at a wedding to the occasions when you are called upon to 'say a few words' or to give a vote of thanks. The knack for cogently presenting an idea or for outlining your reasoning in the face of opposition can be learnt and I offer suggestions on how to achieve this. Many meetings are poorly chaired and a massive amount of time is lost as speakers go round and round in circles. I show you how to chair meetings successfully so that even when you are not officially 'in the chair' you will be able to gently move proceedings along and achieve a positive result.

The earlier edition was written primarily for business professionals because the need to present effectively has become an essential business skill, and I have also updated this area. Many employers now expect candidates for job vacancies to give short presentations at their second interviews so that they can be assessed on their ability to communicate clearly and concisely. If you are facing a change of job or even applying for your first employment this book will certainly help you prepare and will give you an edge over other applicants.

I firmly believe that everyone has the ability to be a good presenter or speaker. Unfortunately, in moments of pressure natural talent flies out of the window and you are left with sweaty palms, a pounding heart and a blank mind. I think I know what changes you from an intelligent, articulate person under normal circumstances, into something else at the very moment when you want to appear at your best, and in this book I show you how to stop this happening.

I founded the International training company Speak First (originally known as SpeakEasy Training) in 1985 because I felt that it was unfortunate that so many people are inhibited and worried about speaking out in public. I have tried to distil my years of training experience into these pages so that you can benefit from them.

Why You Need This Book

Many people confuse public speaking with speaking in public. For me the first is formal and to a large audience while the latter is what most of us are doing every day in some form or other. Here are some examples of the types of occasion that could engage you in public speaking, and for which you may need advice.

- Sitting at meetings and wanting to ask questions but feeling too shy.

- You've recently joined a fund-raising committee and been elected to a residents' association, and would like to learn how to participate more.

- You have to face a bank manger to get a loan or funding for a business venture and feel that you cannot do yourself justice.

- You are about to start a new job and feel your colleagues are more articulate and experienced than you.

- You are about to change jobs and want to know how to prepare a presentation in case that is part of the assessment process.

- You are about to get married and intend to speak at your wedding. (Bear in mind that it is becoming more common for women as well as men to do this.)

- When you present ideas at work you are not paid sufficient attention and you'd like to be more persuasive.

- You are considering running a training course on your own area of expertise.

- You have been promoted and are now required to speak to the media.

How to Use This Book

I have divided the book into three sections so that it is easy to follow. The first part deals mostly with what you want to say and the second half is more about you, the presenter or speaker. Chapter 3 covers preparation for business presentations, and although the principles are often similar for both, Chapter 4 is devoted to talks that are not related to business and how to tackle them. It is often most productive to use a book of this nature as a workbook and apply the guidelines to an actual presentation or talk. In this way you will immediately see how practical and time-saving these techniques can be.

You may already be experienced in presenting to small groups and want to develop your knowledge of other audiences; the third part of the book answers most of your questions and enables you to face either large conferences or inquisitive journalists.

Nobody Is a 'Born Speaker'

We all admire speakers who can casually deliver a humorous, intelligent and well-reasoned talk apparently without trying. However, what might seem to be effortless may well be founded on days and even weeks of editing and practice. The art is to talk so that it appears to be natural. Unfortunately novice speakers often see these 'natural' speakers and are surprised that they cannot achieve the same professional level with their first attempt.

Effective speaking is a skill that can be learnt. You can learn how to select essential points to persuade successfully, to structure a talk so that your listeners will follow you easily and not be bored, to hide nerves and uncertainty and to show enthusiasm and sincerity. In addition, you can learn to develop an interesting speaking voice, make natural gestures and good eye contact, use visual aids and even cope with difficult questions. Nobody was born a good speaker. Bear in mind the words of Emerson, the American author and philosopher: 'All the great speakers were bad speakers first.'

PART ONE

Preparation

1

What is Communication?

'The spoken word belongs half to the one who speaks it and half to the one who hears it.'

FRENCH PROVERB

Poor Listening

What exactly is communication? It's a *two-way* process, so to be an effective speaker it's useful to understand how people listen. If you don't, you could be broadcasting on the wrong frequency and you wouldn't realise it – your message may be clear and powerful, but is it being received?

Unfortunately few people concentrate sufficiently when they are listening so they become distracted, often by their own thoughts. This is sometimes called 'going down Route 350'. Let me explain. It has been estimated that the human mind processes words at a rate of approximately 500 a minute, but that we listen at about 150 words a minute – the difference between the two is 350. When listeners 'switch off', the chances are that they are on Route 350. If you are sitting in a long, tedious meeting you may be thinking about what you want to do at the weekend, while you are listening, or should I say half listening, to what is being said by a speaker. You are going down Route 350.

Sometimes you're distracted because of something the speaker says. They may suggest something you feel is unacceptable and you use your spare brain capacity to work out counter-arguments. Once again, you've set off down Route 350.

Most listeners are not like dry sponges ready to absorb everything the speaker gives them. They are continually assessing, digesting, rejecting or accepting what they hear. They are measuring it against their own bank of experience and prejudice and evaluating its worth. Is this going to work? Is that logical? What happens if I agree? Is this credible? They are judging not only the content of what the speaker is saying, but also the speaker. Why are they saying this? What's their experience? Do they seem to know what they're talking about?

Listeners therefore sometimes fail to concentrate and are distracted by their own thoughts, which may be unrelated to the speaker, or by what they are saying. They may also be distracted by the speaker's behaviour or appearance – thinking that they like her shoes, for example, or asking themselves why he is taking off his glasses.

Reasons for Ineffective Listening

You may begin to wonder whether there is any point in your attempting to speak if no one is likely to listen to you, but bear with me because in the next section I describe the advantages of being a speaker.

For the moment, though, here are some other reasons why people may not be giving you their full attention whether you are addressing a group or talking one to one:

- They anticipate what is going to be said and switch off.

- They are planning what to say when it's their turn.

- They may be tired or worried, i.e. they may have too much on their mind to concentrate.

- They can't hear or they find your voice dull and monotonous.

- The topic is too complex and difficult to follow or it is too simple and basic.

- You lack credibility, confidence and structure, and use too much jargon.

- The chairs are hard; it's either too hot or too cold; and the sound of the traffic is very distracting!

Is Writing a More Effective Communication Channel?

If you didn't speak, how else could you communicate? Maybe by sign language but probably by writing; so what's the difference between speaking and writing?

The major difference is that speakers can see their listeners. As a writer I can't see you, but I'd like to know whether you are still reading this section or whether you have skipped forwards to another chapter. Because speakers can see their listeners, they can react to them. I can't react to you if you disagree with what you've read; I can't give you any additional examples or different arguments to convince you of my point.

Although readers have the freedom to absorb the author's message at their own pace and are able to reread complex passages, the author's words can't be changed to satisfy the readers' needs. By contrast, a speaker has the *flexibility* to alter and vary their message for different listeners. Complex ideas can be re-explained using alternative words and phrases. The advantages and disadvantages of a course of action can be repeated giving a variety of examples. The listeners' own experiences can be used as support for the speaker's argument.

Your funny email might be misunderstood; your letter may go into the waste-paper basket; the recommendations in your report may be ignored, but if you present the same message in person, you are in a stronger position to ensure that it is understood, acknowledged and acted upon.

How to Make a Positive Impression as a Speaker

Although there are advantages in being present when you deliver your message, there are also pitfalls. Inexperienced speakers generally rely too heavily on words, probably because they feel more confident when writing than when speaking, so that they overlook other factors that give a successful speaker impact.

The packaging of your message is important and in situations where there is a mismatch between how you behave and what you are saying people will believe the behaviour rather than the words. It has been estimated by Professor Albert Mehrabian, the communications researcher, that words account for only 7 per cent of the speaker's effect on an audience when there is a mismatch. A massive 55 per cent of the speaker's impact comes from the visual, i.e. how they look, facial expression, gestures, body language and posture, etc.; while 38 per cent of the impact comes from voice. Does the speaker sound trustworthy? Is the speaker's voice varied and interesting to listen to? This breakdown of the effect that a speaker has on a listener may sound unlikely to you. So, imagine a situation where you have returned a faulty item to a store. The shop assistant says, 'I'm sorry. I'll see what we can do.' If this is said in a disinterested voice as the assistant leans on the counter about to resume a conversation with another assistant you won't feel confident that very much will happen. On the other hand, the same words expressed with concern by an assistant who is standing up straight and looking directly at you will create an entirely different impression.

Here is another example. Think back to your favourite teacher or tutor at school or university. The first person who comes to mind is probably someone who was enthusiastic and animated; not a person who only relied on words, but also someone with vocal and visual impact.

If you feel you usually don't notice very much about a speaker's voice, try recalling any phone calls you've made to people who are unknown to you. I am sure you made judgements and assessments based on their voices – she sounded friendly or angry or ineffectual; he was aggressive or honest or happy. Most of the time you will find you are making these evaluations of people unconsciously.

In the same way listeners make evaluations of speakers. They might say, 'He seemed ill at ease' or 'She looked very confident.' Often these opinions are formed before the speaker has said one word and are based entirely on the visual impact. Some people look inspiring and enthusiastic, while others appear dull and insipid. Based on this visual impression listeners will have made up their minds as to whether it's worthwhile paying attention to them.

So, remember that *how* you speak is often as important as what you say. A sound and well-reasoned argument can be ruined by bad delivery, while a poorly constructed or unoriginal talk seems entertaining and convincing if presented with vitality.

Different Techniques: Writing Versus Speaking

Throughout this book, I draw the distinction between speaking and writing because it's often wrongly assumed that the skills of writing can be applied to speaking. If you are aware of the difference between listening and reading you will be able to adjust your approach and successfully reach your audience.

Writer	Speaker
• Writer can't see reader.	• Speaker can see listener.
• Writer can't react.	• Speaker can slow down/ speed up/repeat and involve listeners.
• Writer relies on words alone.	• Speaker can use body language and voice for emphasis, enthusiasm and emotion.
• Writer can use carefully chosen words, but cannot change them.	• Speaker can be more flexible and relevant by modifying and altering words and phrases to suit the listeners.
• Writer explains topic only once and reader can reread.	• Speaker must have a simple, easy-to-follow structure, frequent summaries and relevant examples because listeners can't relisten.

A Final Thought

After a ten-minute talk listeners will have understood and retained approximately half of what was said and a couple of days later they'll only remember about a quarter.

SUMMARY

- Practise your listening skills and learn how to become a more effective listener particularly in situations where you disagree with the speaker. This could be an exercise that you practise at home.

- Remember that a speaker has the flexibility to alter their message for different audiences.

- Aim to create a positive impression and keep in mind that *how* you speak is as important as what you say.

2

Hassle-free Preparation and Planning

'I am the most spontaneous speaker in the world because every word, every gesture, and every retort has been carefully rehearsed.'
GEORGE BERNARD SHAW

In this chapter I describe the process of preparing a presentation and although I have geared it mostly to business presentations many of the steps can be applied equally successfully to talks in social or non-business environments. By the end of the chapter you will have gained an insight into how to prepare a talk employing a logical and easy-to-use framework.

How to Start

The deadline approaches and you finally sit down, determined to start preparing your talk, unable to find any more excuses for putting it off. You search for inspiration and desperately seek an opening line. Alternatively, you may start with your visual aids. If you're preparing for a large meeting, you may skim through a book of jokes because humour is supposed to 'warm up' the audience, but nothing seems appropriate. You may try three or four different opening paragraphs that all end up in the waste-paper bin. I'm not surprised, because you are starting in the wrong place.

Proper preparation and practice prevent poor performance.

Researching Your Audience

Giving a presentation is like going on a journey. Before you start you need to consider your fellow travellers, because paths that may be suitable for one group may be inappropriate for another, and you will lose them before you reach your destination.

You may be reading this book because you need to speak at departmental meetings of eight people, or you may anticipate addressing a conference of 80 or 800 participants. Therefore throughout the rest of the book, I use the word 'audience' to describe *anyone* who is listening to you speak. You may feel that a group of your workmates doesn't constitute an audience, but if you are speaking to them at a business meeting, that is exactly what they are.

Whether your audience is large or small, if you're going to be an effective speaker, you must find out as much as possible about them. Have you ever had the experience of listening to a talk where nothing that the speaker said was relevant to you? You found the material unoriginal and self-evident and from the shuffling and inattentive audience, you judged that others felt the same as you. In fact, there was probably nothing wrong with the talk at all; it was simply given to the wrong audience.

You can toss a cricket ball at a dartboard and hit the bull's eye, but it won't stick. In the same way, you may be speaking well, but is it sticking? Are you using the right words for your listeners? Are you structuring what you have to say so that they will understand easily? Are your illustrations relevant? Deciding whether to throw a cricket ball, a dart, a javelin or even a hammer is one of the skills of speaking. Choosing what you're going to throw depends on what you want to hit.

A group of bank managers asked me to advise them on the presentations they were giving to school leavers. Naturally they hoped to encourage these young men and women to open bank accounts, but somehow they weren't having the success they hoped for. It was hardly surprising. These middle-aged men didn't realise the need to understand their audience. It was no good talking about security, savings and pensions to a group of people who were longing to spend, spend, spend. Once the bank managers made their talk *relevant* to eighteen-year-olds, their presentations were successful.

Finding out about your audience will enable you to make your talk relevant to them and thereby overcome many of the difficulties that listeners face when trying to follow the spoken word: you should plan your journey according to your fellow travellers.

What you need to know about your audience

You know why you are speaking, but do *they*? Ask yourself the following questions:

- Why are they there?

- What do they expect?

- What do they want or need?

- What's their level of knowledge?

- What is their attitude likely to be to you and your views?

• Have they any past experiences that will influence them towards or against you?

When you are speaking to larger, external audiences, you will need to find out additional information, as set out below.

Why are they there?

If you're speaking at a meeting in your own workplace it is possible your audience has no choice about attending: they are there because it's the Friday afternoon meeting; or because there is a threat that a major client is going to move their account; or it's the distribution department's monthly meeting.

Sometimes you have invited your audience to listen to you – for example, you are making a sales presentation to a prospective customer. Alternatively, a client may have asked you to give a progress report on their project. At a public conference, your audience may have paid to attend.

Ask yourself whether your audience have chosen to listen to you and are there of their own free will, or whether they were sent – this can make a significant difference in their attitude towards you. Occasionally I find myself facing a group of antagonistic managers who feel resentful that they have been sent on yet another useless course when they have a desk full of problems to be solved. They are not receptive to my training and begrudge the time wasted on the course. When I am aware of this attitude I try to overcome it.

What do they expect?

You must satisfy your audience's expectations – if they are expecting a report on your experience with flexitime for office staff, telling them about the problems you have finding a suitable garage to service the company vans will not be relevant. A group of business people expecting a light-hearted after-lunch talk will not welcome a plea for more money to be spent on training for young people in industry. In both cases the audience might well be interested in the alternative talk, but if it is not what they were expecting, they will not be receptive listeners.

When a client engages me to teach effective speaking, I know I can spend an amusing morning telling them of some of the disasters I have faced in my speaking career. It would be entertaining but inappropriate if they were expecting to be taught; they might learn from my mistakes, but I would not be teaching them.

Beware of confusing your objective with your audience's expectations. They are not the same. A travel agent client gave a presentation in which he identified his objective as: 'To convince the audience that Spain has more interesting holiday resorts than Greece.' He started his talk by saying: 'I'm going to convince you that ...' No audience wants to be *told* that. They want to make up their own minds. In the above example the audience wanted to be informed about the relative merits of Greek and Spanish holiday resorts. The speaker may be certain of convincing them, but the audience resents being told so, and will erect a mental barrier against the speaker's arguments. A better start might have been: 'I'd like to give you information about Spain and Greece to help you decide which is most attractive for you.'

What do they want or need?

To achieve your objective, or reach your destination with all your fellow travellers, you must make the journey relevant to them. Your message must satisfy their needs. This doesn't mean that you change the content of your message, but simply that you put yourself in your audience's shoes and present it from their point of view.

I once heard a manager arguing that his mobile phone should be upgraded because all the other managers on his grade had a better one. His request was refused. He didn't think about the listener's needs. He should have pointed out to his boss that currently he often missed important email messages as his mobile couldn't receive them, and that on occasions he had arrived at cancelled meetings because he hadn't seen the email advising of the cancellation. He could have said: 'My wasted time is costing you a lot of money – with a new mobile I would be more efficient.'

In general you can be fairly sure that one or more of the management needs listed below should be satisfied by your argument:

- saving money;
- increasing productivity and efficiency;
- saving time;
- improving quality.

If you are talking to your workforce, you may find that other needs are paramount:

- earning more money;
- recognition of work effort;
- security of employment;
- job satisfaction;
- career advancement.

This is by no means a complete list; you'll be able to identify the needs of your own audience when you start to think about them in this way.

I once had to advise a local government client who was unable to convince applicants for grants of the importance of accurate form filling. Each form submitted had miscalculations, omissions and incorrect information, which were causing more work for everyone concerned. Although the applicants had been told several times that the forms were important, they continued to fill them in with careless mistakes. I suggested the client look at it from the applicants' point of view. What did they want? What were their needs? The answer was that the applicants wanted their grants as quickly as possible. The next question was how to satisfy this need. The answer, of course, was by accurate form filling; and the client went on to explain how this could be achieved. When the applicants were shown how they could benefit from following the instructions, they were prepared to listen.

If you are facing an unwilling audience, you'll need to tell them at the beginning of your talk how they will benefit from listening to you. In order to do this, you must, of course, know their needs. I tell reluctant managers on my courses that I can show them how to save time preparing their talks; how they need never fear boring an audience; how I can teach them to overcome nervousness; and how they can look and sound more professional. At the end of this little speech, I hope I have gained their attention and overcome their reluctance to be there.

What's their level of knowledge?

Here are some more questions you must ask as part of your audience research:

- How much do they already know about the topic?

- How much do they think they know?

- How much do they want to know?

- How much do they need to know so that you achieve the result you want?

The last question is the most important, but you can only answer it when you have some idea of the knowledge they have already.

If you were explaining how new legislation could affect your company, you would choose a different starting point when addressing the personnel director than when talking to the warehouse manager. You may have been part of an audience or group at which the speaker assumed a common background knowledge which *you* didn't have and consequently you found it difficult to follow the arguments. Alternatively, if you were familiar with a subject, it would be equally irritating to listen to fulsome explanations. In both situations, the speaker has not done sufficient audience research, and it is impossible to make the message relevant and prevent listeners wandering off down Route 350. The uninformed group will try to fathom out the speaker's meaning; the more knowledgeable one will be bored by the content.

In a situation where you are aware that there will be a varied level of knowledge, you can give enough background information to enable everyone to understand your talk – for example, 'You'll probably remember that the dip in sales revenue last October was due to the cancellation of the large Australian order. I think we need to bear this in mind when looking at these figures.'

Avoid using phrases like: 'For the benefit of those who don't know ...' or 'For the less experienced among you ...' No one wants to be identified (even to themselves) as one of the ignorant.

What is their attitude likely to be to you and your views?

In favour? Against? Indifferent? Open-minded?

If, before you speak, you are aware of any negative attitudes, you can attempt to overcome objections within your talk: 'You may be wondering how we can achieve this without taking on more staff ...' or 'If this sounds like an expensive proposal, may I suggest you look at it this way ...' or 'Many people say I look too young to have enough experience to cope with the problems of this department ...'

Have they any past experiences that will influence them towards or against you?

Bad experiences colour people's judgements and often create invisible barriers that prevent your message from being received and understood. You must acknowledge and remove such obstacles if you are to reach your destination with your listeners: 'I know that a similar experiment using temporary staff failed last year, but let me show you how my scheme is different,' 'Some of you may have given up using an outside contractor because of the communication problems that it posed. We can prevent this happening by ...'

Checklist for speaking to external audiences

On occasion you may be asked to speak outside your own workplace as a panellist, a guest speaker or a workshop leader chairing a discussion, or as an after-lunch or dinner speaker. The more you can discover about the audience and the location, the more confident and effective you will be as a speaker. This checklist will help you.

Who?

Find out about your audience; ask your contact all the specific questions listed below:

* How many will be present?

* What is their position/occupation/title?

* What is their background/education/culture/race?

* What is their sex, male/female/male and female?

* What is their age?

Where?

Make sure you know the exact address and telephone number, available parking, nearest railway station/airport. What type of room/hall/office/conference centre will you be in?

When?

What is the day of the week, the date and the exact time?

What?

What are the topic and any specific angle, as well as the reason for inviting you?

How?

Will there be a stage/lectern? Is there a microphone and, if so, what type? What equipment is available? How will the audience be sitting? In rows/a semi-circle/with tables?

Duration?

How long should you speak and does this include question time? When will the questions be taken? Will there be a panel discussion?

Other speakers?

Names and telephone numbers of any other speakers would be useful.

See also Chapter 16 on writing and reading scripts for conferences for more advice on this topic.

Setting an Objective

Now you have researched your fellow travellers, you can concentrate on your destination. You need to know where you are heading and where you want to get to – in other words, what is the objective of your presentation? Later, you choose your path, but if you don't know where you are going, it is difficult to decide how to get there.

Before you even consider what you want to say, ask yourself, 'Why am I speaking?' What do you want to achieve? How do you want your listeners to feel when you have finished? What is the reaction you most want from your audience? Allow yourself to daydream about the ideal outcome of your talk. Don't worry about whether it's likely, or even possible, at this stage; simply identify what you want to accomplish.

Sometimes clients find it difficult to pinpoint exactly what they want to achieve. They tell me: 'I'm speaking because it's the annual sales conference,' 'I'm speaking because I've been told to,' 'I'm speaking because I am the Chairman,' 'I'm speaking because it's my turn,' and so on. If you are unsure how to identify your objectives, here are some pointers.

Start with general objectives

General objectives fall into the following categories:

- to inform/teach/train;
- to stimulate/motivate/inspire;
- to persuade/convince/sell;
- to explore/debate/negotiate;
- to amuse/entertain.

Writing down your objective in clear, precise terms is often difficult, but if you refer to the general objectives, they should help you. Remember that you will sometimes need to combine several objectives. When I speak to the personnel team of a large company about my training courses, my objective is *to sell* training to them. However, I also *inform* them of the content of the courses, *inspire* them with stories of previous successes, *motivate* them by showing them how economical our training is compared with that of other companies, *persuade* them with logical arguments and even *shame* them by pointing out how poorly their company's staff perform compared with staff of other organisations. Remember that one general objective should predominate; don't confuse yourself with a mixture of too many general objectives, but always aim to include some entertainment.

Do write out your objective. Remember it must be *specific*, but also *achievable*. If your objective is to convince your boss that you should have a company car (which may be an achievable objective), don't insist that it should be a Rolls-Royce (probably an unachievable objective).

I advised a hospital manager on a speech she was giving to a convention of doctors. She was concerned that she had nothing new to say and that she would bore her audience. She was unable to find the means to straighten out a jumble of thoughts until I asked her what changes in their behaviour she would like to inspire. Suddenly she saw how she could prepare a very passionate speech on doctors' attitudes towards nursing staff. Once she had an objective her thoughts became directed and fell into a logical sequence. When she had decided her destination, she was able to choose her route to it.

Another client, a managing director of a family-owned business, annually 'addressed the troops' (his words). Each year he spoke for twenty minutes and although for many of his staff this was the only occasion when they saw him, most of them considered it to be a boring waste of time. I asked him how he would like his staff to feel after he had spoken. For some time he talked vaguely of motivation and productivity and feeling happy at work and finally he said he wanted them to understand how much he genuinely needed them. We then started to look at how he could achieve this. He had a destination, so he could start examining the various paths that might lead there.

You may be saying to yourself that that's all very well for anyone who needs to speak in public, but you only need to speak at internal meetings. I suggest that, before your next meeting, you set aside a few minutes to think about objectives and answer the question, what do you want to accomplish by speaking? Is it to convince colleagues that your ideas are better than theirs? Do you want to stimulate a sales force? Maybe you want to impress your boss. Be honest and find your real objective. It should be:

- written down;
- specific;
- achievable.

Where's the action?

As you set out your objective, be sure to identify exactly what you want to achieve and how you will measure whether or not you have been successful. Sometimes an *action* will follow. In selling, you know you have achieved your objective when the customer agrees to buy. You also can have a fall-back position or a *secondary objective*; you may not make a sale, but your customer gives you the names of several companies which might be interested in your product. Your boss may not agree to a company car immediately, but does agree to you having one in six months.

You may find that identifying the reaction you want from your listeners helps you to set an objective. I talked to a manager who had been asked to speak at a convention which was to be attended by politicians, members of the press and senior representatives of his industry. He was uncertain what he should say, so I asked what he would like them to do as a result of what he had said. He found lots of actions, so he started from the action and worked backwards. To identify the action, you must ask yourself how you want people *to behave* or what you want people *to do* after they have heard you speak. An office supervisor may identify the action he requires as 'a decrease in the number of telephone calls put through to the wrong extensions'. His objectives might eventually look like this:

- to instruct the switchboard operators on the new telephone equipment;

- to motivate them to take a pride in their job so that fewer phone calls are put through to the wrong extensions.

He would be able to measure whether he had been successful by monitoring the phone calls two weeks after his presentation. Remember to include a method of measuring whether you have achieved your objective or not.

When you have completed this first stage of your preparation, you should have a clear and concisely written objective which answers the question:

> *Why am I speaking and what do I want the outcome to be?*

You might be tempted to skip this step as it can be time-consuming to write down a succinctly worded objective that is achievable and honest and measurable. However, the time and effort you spend on objective setting now will be saved later on in your preparation as it will be easier to select material and identify key points.

Brainstorm Your Ideas

So far in your preparation you've discovered as much as you can about your fellow travellers and you have chosen your destination. Your next step is to study the map. What routes will be most effective in helping you reach your destination? What material should you include in your talk to help you achieve your objective?

You may need to speak in a variety of different situations, but the method I describe for researching your material can probably be applied equally well to all of them. From now on

I refer to your 'talk', although you may actually be making a presentation, giving instructions, leading a training group, presenting a report or making a speech.

When you have been asked to give a talk, the usual reaction is 'Why me? I don't have anything to say.' When the initial panic has died down, you'll probably realise that you have a great deal to say and your real problem is deciding what to leave out.

Freeing the mind

I expect most of your original ideas come to you at inconvenient moments like driving on the motorway in the fast lane, under the shower or in the middle of the night. I'm going to show you a method of capturing interesting ideas when it's most convenient for you.

Unfortunately, much of our education has trained us to think in a logical and linear manner. As you sit in front of your computer or with a blank piece of paper in front of you to prepare your talk, you may even start with a (i) in the margin, but most ideas don't arrive in a numbered sequence; it's difficult if not impossible to be creative and structured at the same time. So, instead of forcing your creativity into a linear structure, draw a circle in the centre of your paper and write in it the subject of your talk and, as you let your mind freewheel around it, jot down any ideas that come to you. Place your ideas on lines radiating from the central topic. You'll find that each idea triggers off others so that you can continuously build on them. The advantage of this mind map (see over) is that you have plenty of space to add new thoughts and you can also expand on those you have already jotted down. You'll have to avoid the temptation to reject material before you have written it down. This is *not* an evaluation exercise. It is simply a method of brainstorming with yourself so you can put on paper everything that you know about your subject. Try not to

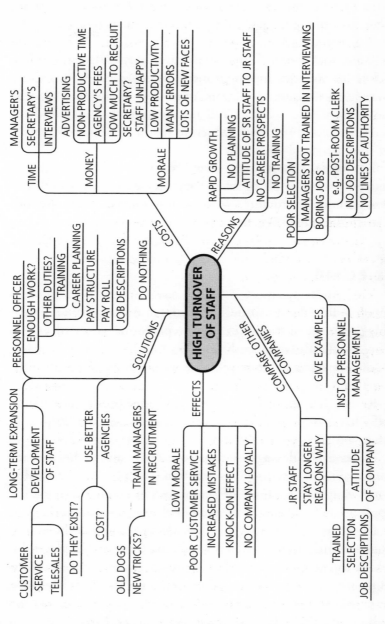

Mind map

assess whether the material is relevant or logical – that can come later. I find that if I build the mind map over several days, new thoughts and angles occur to me at odd moments during that period.

Sometimes when I suggest a mind map to clients, they dislike the concept, finding it messy or confused. At this stage that doesn't matter. It's more important to follow through thoughts, views, opinions and information that may lead to examples and illustrations, which in turn will help your listeners to understand your talk.

Too often people curb their creativity when they judge material as unsuitable or when they decide that it doesn't fit a predetermined structure. With a mind map, there are no restrictions, and every idea and thought has equal merit.

Selection

If you didn't like the untidiness of the mind map, you'll probably prefer the next stage in your preparation. Now look at the map and decide which paths or ideas are most suitable for your fellow travellers so that you can all reach your destination together.

Revisit your objective and your audience profile. Ask yourself what material you need to achieve your objective, knowing what you do about the audience.

Assess each idea against your objective, always bearing in mind your audience's likely reaction. An idea that is totally convincing for a group of senior businessmen may not be appropriate for young male and female graduate trainees.

I once heard a sales trainer advising a predominantly female audience that rugby and cricket clubs were useful places in which to extend their range of contacts. Good advice maybe, but not necessarily for that audience. Your first criterion must be to select material that is relevant to your audience, and that will make it easier for you to achieve your objective.

Secondly, refer back to your audience's needs. How can you satisfy them? Can you present your report in such a way as to show that your recommendations will save the company money? Can you persuade your staff to accept the new schedules by offering them greater job satisfaction? Are you addressing a large audience consisting of people who want to achieve recognition in their own field? Any audience will want to know what's in it for them, so select material that will satisfy their needs and their expectations.

Be very selective

If you overload your talk with too many good points, your audience will forget them all. Remember that after a couple of days they will only have retained approximately a quarter of what you have said. You will be more effective if you choose one or two points, develop them, present supporting evidence, choose relevant illustrations, and recap and summarise frequently.

SUMMARY

- Who is going to listen? Find out as much as you can about the audience.

- Try brainstorming a mind map. Avoid assessing at this stage – simply be creative.

- Be very selective by choosing a few key points to achieve your objective.

- In other words, get to know your fellow travellers, choose your destination, study the map and finally choose the paths that will take you there together without losing anyone on the way.

3

Structuring an Easy-to-follow Presentation

'Good order is the foundation of all things.'
EDMUND BURKE (*Reflections on the Revolution in France*, 1790)

In this chapter I describe how to choose a logical structure to help your listeners follow your talk, how to develop key ideas and how to add supporting material, including illustrations and examples. By the end of the chapter you should be able to construct a persuasive and entertaining talk or presentation.

Organise Your Main Points

Listeners find it difficult to concentrate on the spoken word, so you must give them a framework. This is the equivalent of chapter headings in the contents page of a book and the sub-headings of paragraphs. If you announce your structure early on in your talk, your listeners will be able to refer back to it if they wander down Route 350 from time to time. By summarising after each of your points, you can lead them back on to the main track with you. Bear in mind that they can't reread your previous paragraph so you need to help them when their concentration fails.

Deciding on a structure

In order to be effective your structure must be logical, simple to follow and relevant to your audience. Here are some types of structure you can use.

Problem/solution

This is a common structure often used in business presentations in which an examination of the problem is followed by a proposed solution. For example, if your department is experiencing a high turnover of staff, you could describe the problem and show how to resolve it by proposing a more selective recruitment programme. If your company has a low profile in the trade press, you could outline the current situation and suggest a public relations campaign to improve its image. A variation on this structure can be used when you are in a competitive bid for a customer's business: describe the problem, examine a number of possible solutions, pointing out the weaknesses of each, and finally present your own solution emphasising all the advantages.

Chronological structure

In this method the key points are given in a natural time-sequence order. For instance, you could state the origins of the product and how it developed over the course of a number of years to meet changing needs. It is also helpful when you are instructing or training, as you can demonstrate the sequence of steps or stages in a particular process. Listeners find it easy to follow a logical time pattern. However, this doesn't allow you to indicate the importance of one idea in relation to another.

Your second and fourth points may be more important than the points preceding them, but this won't be apparent from the order in which you present them. You can rectify this disadvantage in your final conclusion by focusing on the areas you feel are most significant.

Topical structure

Also known as the qualitative structure, when you use the topical structure you list your points in their order of significance with the most important at the beginning. This is useful when you think your audience may not concentrate through your entire talk and are likely to pay more attention in the first few minutes. Generally, the listener's attention is keenest at the beginning of a talk and therefore it's prudent to take advantage of this. Remember that, in selecting your most telling or important idea, you must refer back to your objective and the needs of the audience.

Spatial structure

In this structure you can either begin with the particular and move to the general or, alternatively, examine the big picture first and then show how it applies to the audience. For example, you may want to analyse the sales pattern for the past six months and then put it into the context of the previous three years. You could present new taxation legislation in broad terms and then explain how it would apply in two situations of particular relevance to the audience.

Theory/practice

With this structure you outline the theory and then show how it works in practice. It's often beneficial to link the theory to what the audience already knows about the subject and then progress on to the less familiar. I once saw a trainer instructing a young group of new employees in basic telephone skills. He asked them to recall situations when they felt they had been treated well on the phone and also occasions when they had had to wait unnecessarily. He checked what impression they had of the companies with which they had been dealing. From their personal experience he was able to demonstrate the importance of dealing efficiently with members of the public on the phone. He went on to show them the techniques they could use in future on the phone, and was able to establish that their role was critical in creating a positive company image.

Finding the correct order

It is helpful to choose a suitable structure at this stage in your preparation, because it enables you to place your ideas in the correct order. If you are undecided on your structure, try writing out your main points on several small cards or Post-it notes so that you can physically move them about and experiment with a variety of different sequences.

Expand and Explain Principal Ideas

The next preparation step will depend on the type of talk you are giving. If you are merely speaking for a few minutes at an internal meeting, you may find that you only need to note down a few selected points from your mind map, choose the sequence that will be most logical for your audience, and your preparation will be complete.

Alternatively, if you are addressing a conference of several hundred people, or bidding for an important contract, you will want to plan in more detail how you can develop and support your main points and present them in the most positive way.

Think around your key ideas. If your colleagues have some experience of the topic, talk to them, as an exchange of views can often stimulate a new train of thought; do write down any of the examples or illustrations that will help you to emphasise a particular point.

Occasionally, when I am preparing a talk, I use a tape recorder at this stage. You might find it useful to imagine that a member of your audience is seated in front of you and you have the opportunity of speaking to that person on a one-to-one basis. Switch on your tape recorder and talk around your key points. At first you will feel inhibited, but persevere as you may find that talking aloud opens up previously untapped areas of material and releases ideas you had stored at the back of your mind. Remember that the purpose of this exercise is to expand the key ideas you have already selected; you should be researching ways of presenting these main points so that your audience is totally involved and persuaded by you. Try to avoid adding new main points at this juncture. A rough guide is one point per five minutes with a maximum of five points in thirty minutes. You should avoid speaking for more than twenty minutes, but if this isn't possible, consider using two or three speakers to add variety.

Each of your key ideas is a mini speech and needs to be introduced, developed and concluded; they should be linked together and should have two or three minor points to support them. If you want to write out your talk, some of the suggestions in Chapter 16 may help you, or you can write down your main points on white cards (see page 118).

Add Colour and Sweeteners

Once you have written or outlined the body of your talk, try to identify where the dull patches occur; you are unlikely to maintain a high level of concentration from your listeners throughout your talk and therefore need to add colour and sweeteners to stimulate their interest. The graph overleaf demonstrates this.

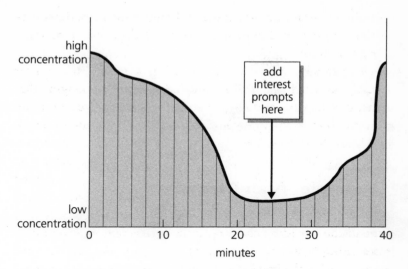

add
interest
prompts
here

Concentration curve of audiences

Aim for a variety of facts, personal illustrations, examples and explanations. It's this mixture that holds an audience's attention. Some of your material may be heavy and difficult to digest, so intersperse it with some real-life examples to make it more acceptable to your audience. Try to break up chunks of essential but dry information with illustrations that are relevant to your listeners. Ask yourself whether some of your points could be better explained with the use of a visual aid. Remember that a visual aid should be a visual expression of an idea that is difficult to describe with words alone. Ask yourself whether your audience would find it easier to follow your talk if they had a handout or a chart or a table of figures to refer to (see also Chapter 6, page 75).

Is there a natural break between two points where it would be worthwhile asking the audience some questions? Are there any other techniques involving the audience that you could use to break up the presentation? See Chapter 18 on interacting with the audience. Even changing your physical position helps the audience to maintain their attention. Too much movement is distracting, but an occasional change of your position from one side of the room or platform to the other enables the audience to refocus.

You only need to consider these suggestions for varying the mixture within your talk if you are speaking for over five minutes. Under this time the content should be sufficient to keep your listeners alert.

Example: Alan Glanville's Presentation

The illustration of the mind map on page 25 shows how one manager brainstormed the problem of a constant turnover of staff that his company faced. On his mind map Alan Glanville jotted down all aspects of the problem, together with his ideas for solving it. He wanted to convince his board of directors that the company needed to employ a trained personnel officer, but he knew that they considered this an unnecessary expense for a company of their size.

Alan decided that a problem/solution structure most suited his ten-minute presentation, but he also wanted to make use of some of the other structures to develop his key points. He felt that, as the overriding objection to employing a personnel officer was financial, he needed to show how much the continual recruitment of staff had cost the company in the past.

- Alan's objective: to convince the board of directors that the company could save time and money and create a happier and more productive workforce by appointing a personnel officer.

- How did he achieve this objective? By demonstrating the real cost of recruiting staff under the present system.

- What action did he want which would indicate that he had achieved his objective? Agreement for him to place an advertisement for a personnel officer.

Below is the outline for Alan's talk showing how he developed each of his key points:

1. The problem

(a) How it developed (chronological structure, past–present)

Small, family-run company with loyal staff; sudden, rapid growth; inadequate job descriptions; poorly recruited new staff; insufficient training; dissatisfaction and low morale among employees.

(b) Cost in time and money of recruiting (spatial structure)

Cost of advertisements; secretary's time handling responses to advertisements; manager's time interviewing candidates; non-productive time for training.

Use a flip chart to show true costs of recruiting one secretary. In one year, twenty junior staff replaced, e.g. post-room clerk changed five times. Show total cost over a twelve-month period of recruiting twenty people.

(c) Why don't staff stay longer? (topical structure)

Poor recruitment because managers not trained as interviewers; unclear lines of authority, e.g. warehouse packing clerk should help post room on busy days, but who decides? Poor job descriptions, e.g. relief work on switchboard done as a favour and causes resentment; no formal wages structure, e.g. pay increases apparently given at the whim of manager, resulting in complaints of favouritism; staff with the company for three years accused of not welcoming newcomers; senior staff don't know names of junior staff.

2. The solution

(d) Personnel officer (chronological structure, present–future)

Show main advantages of solving the current problem; overcome any objections regarding costs, i.e. refer to the high cost of recruiting new staff. Other advantages: some departments will be more productive as aspects of their present work will be handled by personnel officer, e.g. accounts department and the pay roll, secretaries will not be involved in recruiting; central pay structure – fewer complaints; proper job descriptions – less friction; recruiting with career development in mind, e.g. customer service department currently handles telephoned complaints, with sales training they could develop telephone-selling skills; long-term planning and expansion easier without present difficulties.

You can see from the above example how Alan selected some of the key ideas and developed them to achieve his objective. He chose to use the flip chart to demonstrate the actual cost of recruiting one secretary, as spoken numbers are difficult to comprehend and retain. If a flip chart hadn't been available, he could have prepared a handout showing a breakdown of his calculations to help his audience follow his arguments.

In order that his presentation should not become too theoretical, he gave several examples and illustrations to make it come alive for his listeners, e.g. changing the post-room clerk five times.

Although all the ideas on his mind map were valid and interesting, you will see that because he wanted to speak only for ten minutes he had to reject some of them, but he made sure that the file that he took to the meeting contained the additional information in case he was asked questions about it.

Later on in this chapter (see pages 43 and 46) you will see how Alan chose to begin and conclude his presentation.

How to Start

You may recall that this was the title of the first section in Chapter 2. As you can see, you need to spend sufficient time and effort on the body of your talk before you reach the stage where you can choose your opening sentences.

Making Your First Impression

In some ways your opening words are the most important because they are assessing how much of their mental energy you deserve. You will already have made a first impression before you actually say a single word and as they hear your voice (maybe for the first time) you will be failing or passing the next test. How interesting are you? Are you worth listening to? Do you have *enthusiasm*, *sincerity* and *vitality*?

Your first few words should cause the audience to prick up their ears and wait for your next sentence. Try to grab their attention and suspend their mental questioning. Aim to make your opening words imaginative, stimulating and above all attention gaining. Don't confuse your opening words with the introduction to your subject. That comes later. If you feel that this sounds too theatrical for your presentation, don't dismiss the concept completely; look at the examples below and consider whether you could use one or several of them to make your next talk more entertaining.

Your opening words to your audience must be enticing and seductive, and should make them want to listen to you. You need to capture their attention, stop their minds wandering and show them you're worth listening to. It's a tall order, but essential if you expect to achieve your objectives.

It's as simple as A, B, C and D:

Attention Capture their attention and stop their thoughts from wandering.

Benefits show them what they will gain from listening – give them a valid reason to pay attention.

Credentials Give them your credentials for speaking – what is your experience of the subject (for audiences who don't know you).

Direction and destination Tell them the structure and chapter headings of your talk.

This may seem a lot to fit into one paragraph, but it can be covered in less than a minute. I have described these four ingredients in more detail below, because from my own experience I know that your opening few sentences can be crucial to the success of your talk.

Attention-getting techniques

Ask a question

- 'Do you know how many phone calls the accounts department receives every day?'

- 'Can you remember what you were doing on Tuesday 11 August last year?'

- 'Have you any idea how many hours you spend in your car each week?'

As you read through those questions, you may have quickly thought of your own answers and that is what the audience does, or else they listen for an answer from the speaker. Questions engage the minds of the audience and make them concentrate. Try not to make your opening question too involved otherwise they will be working out the answer and won't be listening to your next sentence; *do* make the question relevant to the audience.

Quotation

- 'The brain is a wonderful organ – it begins working the moment you are born and goes on working perfectly until the moment that you have to stand up and speak in public.'

- 'There are two kinds of men who never amount to much; those who cannot do what they are told and those who can do nothing else.'

- 'Doing business without advertising is like winking in the dark – you know what you are doing but no one else does.'

You can spend hours in bookshops or on the Internet looking for an appropriate opening for your talk. Many collections of quotations are compiled by subject and this reduces your research time. Some quotes benefit from your giving their source and you can preface your remark something along the lines of, 'I like the advice that Mark Twain gave on public speaking "The right word may be effective, but no word can ever be as effective as a mighty, timed pause."' If you hear another speaker with a pithy and amusing quotation, note it down and keep it on file so that you can refer to it when you get stuck. Everyone knows that recycling is good for the environment.

Anecdotes

A short story that launches you quickly into the subject matter of your talk is useful, provided it is relevant to the audience and to your topic. Here is an extract from a story I heard at a meeting of personnel managers in which the speaker introduced his talk by describing the impossibly high expectations of some of the applicants for a recently advertised job:

> One young man said that he liked the sound of the job but that at his last employment he was paid more and the conditions were better. I asked him what they were and he told me that he was given free life insurance, was enrolled in a private health scheme, every year was given a 10 per cent bonus at Christmas, had six weeks' paid holiday a year and free travel, and every Friday they finished at 3 p.m. I said to him, 'It sounds perfect, why on earth did you leave?' He looked at me sheepishly and said, 'They went bust.'

On another occasion I heard a speaker open his talk on business acumen with this true story:

> Once upon a time there were two soft drinks companies. One got into deep financial trouble and the other was offered the opportunity to buy them out. The successful company figured the unsuccessful one couldn't last long and turned down the takeover opportunity. The successful company was Coca-Cola and the other one was Pepsi. Somewhere someone must be kicking himself.

If you are using second-hand material, try to personalise it so that it appears to be your own experience. It is generally best to use your own stories, provided you cut out any irrelevant detail. In Chapter 13 on using humour, you'll see that the most successful anecdotes are those you tell against yourself.

Shock openings

These can be fun, but you must be confident and deliver your words carefully so that their full impact is felt by the audience. For instance, try: 'You are wasting your time sitting here listening to me [pause] unless you're prepared to act on my suggestions.' Here is another: 'There is an epidemic in Britain that can't be cured by doctors but it's responsible for more lost worker-hours in British industry than any other. Doctors can't cure it, but we can. I'm talking about backache.'

Historical background

This is a suitable beginning to set the context for a speech with a chronological structure: 'Twenty years ago this hall was a field and the idea for an industrial estate was being ferociously debated in the Town Hall.'

Current affairs

Sometimes a news item provides the right peg on which to hang your talk. Be careful not to use an item that has only just appeared in the news bulletins, as your listeners may not have heard of it. You can find this opening useful if you are visiting a town and you refer to a local story; your audience will feel that you are taking an interest in their area and not just passing through. However, remember to comment in a favourable way.

The benefits – what's in it for them?

Once you have gained your listeners' attention, you must tell them why they should continue to listen to you. In other words, show them what's in it for them. This only needs a few words, but it reinforces the impression that you are worth their mental energy. Refer back to your audience research to find out what their needs and wants are, because when you describe the benefit it must be specific to them.

Here is an example of how a general manager began his talk when he was addressing a sales conference: 'We are going to double your commission and halve your targets this year. You may think that I have got that round the wrong way. I'm going to describe a new product that is so good that you'll only need to put in half the effort for twice the rewards.'

At a client presentation the manager of a mailing house company described to her client how she had reduced a competitor's mailing costs by half and promised that she could do the same for them.

In both these instances the audience may only half believe what they hear but nevertheless they are prepared to pay attention to the speaker. I had the experience of attending a conference for trainers where one of the speakers told us that she could show us how to save an hour a day if we followed her method of time management. I certainly wanted an extra hour in my day and so I could see the benefit in listening to what she had to say.

Credentials – establish your credibility

In your next sentence you should tell your audience why you are qualified to speak on that subject, in other words, what your experience is. A few words usually suffice to demonstrate that you are the right person. For instance, a systems analyst was addressing a school board. 'During the last four years I have personally supervised the computerisation of records in eight large schools in the region so I understand the kind of problems that you are facing here.' At an insurance investigators' conference a speaker explained his experience to the audience like this: 'While I was in the States I researched the methods being used there to detect fraud in insurance claims so that I am now in a position to compare their methods with ours.'

You can use your opening sentences to establish a rapport with the audience and possibly overcome any prejudices which they may have towards you, as this speaker did: 'Like you, I have not been to university but I have done every job in this factory, so you can be sure I'm not going to suggest any changes that won't work.' By reaching out towards the audience, the speaker was helping them to accept his proposals.

Direction – give them a route map

Tell your audience what you are going to say, say it and then tell them you've said it. The audience wants to know what's coming and it will make it easier for them to follow your talk if you share your map with them. It's not necessary to be very formal in this, as you will see from this extract from a warehouse manager's talk: 'I have two suggestions that I hope will show you how we can improve the layout of our stores department.' A distribution manager chose to preface her talk like this: 'The problem of incorrect deliveries has to be tackled in three ways. One, why do they occur? Two, what can we do to stop them? And three, how much will it cost?'

Alan's presentation

Here are the four opening sentences of Alan's presentation to the Board:

'Junior staff are costing this company five times as much as our competitors. Why? Because none of them are staying more than six months and some are leaving after only a few weeks.' (Attention getter)

'I'm going to suggest how we can reduce that cost and increase our efficiency.' (Benefits)

'During the last month I've talked to every department manager as well as many personnel managers outside the company, so I think I know what will work for us and what won't.' (Credentials)

'I want to cover four areas. First I'd like to look at how this problem has developed, second how much it costs us, third why staff don't stay longer, and fourth what we can do about it.' (Direction)

Closing Sentences

Your listeners' attention will always be at its highest at the beginning and end of your talk, so you must take advantage of this and conclude with a positive restatement of your message. You will sometimes see an apparently confident speaker suddenly mutter a quick thank you and sit down abruptly. This gives the impression that the speaker can't wait to finish what was an unpleasant experience. There is no need to thank the audience and often these words are only used to help the speaker get off the stage and out of the limelight.

Your conclusion shouldn't come as a surprise. It should be predictable in order to allow the audience to pay maximum attention. It should be brief and not include any new material.

Below are listed some of the ways in which you can end decisively.

Summarise

Use phrases like 'in conclusion', 'to sum up' or 'finally', to indicate that you are about to finish. Be sure to end shortly after these words – don't continue for another five minutes.

Ask for action

You can summarise and tell the audience what you expect them to do: 'I think you'll agree, having heard what I've said, that we must increase the budget for this project. Therefore I am asking you to vote for the increase.'

Ask a question

You may want to leave the audience with a question. This is particularly effective when you have posed a problem and have offered a solution: 'The question is not whether we can afford to increase our budget but whether we can afford *not* to. The decision is with you; what do you think?'

Use a quotation

Once again a good source of quotations will provide an ending that is humorous or profound, depending on the mood you want to create: 'Lord Mancroft once said that a speech is like a love affair. Any fool can start it, but to end it requires considerable skill.'

Tell an anecdote

A story told at the end of a talk must be short and emphasise the main theme of what you have been stressing. Remember to personalise it and make it relevant to your audience. After a recent talk on career development to a group of women managers I told them this story: 'Women are in a stronger position than ever before – even my young nephew has recognised this. He came home recently and told his father that he was second in class. First place was held by a girl. "Surely you're not going to be beaten by a mere girl," said his father. "Well you see," said my nephew, "girls are not as mere as they used to be."'

Alan's presentation

Alan ended his presentation by summarising his recommendation and asking for action:

'So in conclusion I recommend we stop spending unnecessary time and money taking on staff who are unsuitable and who leave after a short time. We need a trained personnel officer. I would like to have your permission to advertise for a personnel officer. In the long run this will cost us less and help to create a happier workforce, which will lead to increased productivity and efficiency.'

SUMMARY

- Once you have collected and researched the content of your presentation select a suitable structure, and add signposts and mini summaries.

- You can expand your key ideas with supporting evidence.

- Try adding colour to the grey patches using relevant examples and personal illustrations.

- Choose a punchy beginning that encourages your audience to listen.

- End decisively and avoid waffle and saying thank you unnecessarily.

4

Social Events and Meetings

In the previous two chapters I described how to prepare and construct a business presentation. In this chapter I suggest how you might go about preparing for other situations, such as weddings, leaving parties, introducing a speaker and giving a vote of thanks. Do refer to the techniques I have mentioned previously, as in same cases they will only need slight modification. I also include guidelines for chairing a meeting successfully.

To speak or not to speak?

One of the problems about many of the occasions at which you may have to speak is that they are emotionally charged, key moments in your life with family and friends present. I am thinking of weddings, funerals, bar mitzvahs, graduations and leaving parties, as well as significant birthdays. I have spoken at most of them, but I was given some good advice by the pastor who officiated at my mother's funeral. He explained that although many people want to acknowledge their loved ones by speaking about them as part of the service, this can distract them from their grieving because their attention will be on their speech rather than on the mourning process.

I think this can be applied to all special occasions that have such a personal element. I remember seeing a sensitive young groom being overcome by his deep feelings and breaking down in tears when he was about to give his speech. In such cases ask yourself whether it is essential that you speak and whether it will interfere with your enjoyment of what should be a great day for you. There are often other people who can speak on your behalf or, as in the case of the young groom, you can limit yourself to a simple, 'Thank you for being here to share this occasion with me.'

Weddings

The traditional English wedding – Scottish, Irish and Welsh weddings are similar – is very different from weddings in other countries. I recall speaking to an Argentinian who was amazed that all the weddings he went to in England followed the same pattern. He thought at first that they had copied the identical style because many of the people involved knew one another. Then he saw the film *Four Weddings and a Funeral* and realised that it was a national phenomenon. Other nationalities, races and creeds do things differently and I have noticed that their influence is affecting how the British do things now.

If you need to plan a big wedding I suggest you look for a book devoted to the subject as here I only give a few pointers about preparing the speeches. You may choose to have no speeches or only one. I attended a second-time-around wedding recently where the grown-up children of the bride and groom 'gave away' their parents and the ceremony was designed from scratch by the participants – this included rewriting the words to the Beatles' song 'Will you still love me when I'm *eighty*-four?'. At a dinner the previous evening the guests were invited to 'say a few words' if they felt inclined, but at the wedding reception only the groom spoke to publicly declare his love for his bride.

Will you take this woman?

The first stage is to decide whether you want a traditional event or to go down the informal and personal route. If it is the latter remember that for your marriage to be legal and recognised in the United Kingdom there are certain formalities that have to be followed, so check before you book the castle in Spain or hot-air balloon flight over the Serengeti, Kenya.

Traditionally there are three men who speak at the wedding reception: the bride's father, the bridegroom and the best man. Nowadays it is not uncommon for the bride to speak, as well as her mother; I have also heard contributions from the groom's father and the best woman, who provides a role to the bride that is similar to the role provided by the best man to the groom. If you decide that all seven should speak you will have to ensure that there is no overlap in what they intend to say, and that they keep their speeches to a strict time limit of less than five minutes. Even then you will probably find that most of them run over and your guests are forced to sit in their places for three-quarters of an hour of speech making!

If you are one of those invited to speak, where should you start? As in the case of any presentation, you need to identify the reason why you are speaking. In the main it will be to thank the various members of the wedding party, congratulate the bride and groom and propose a toast.

The **bride's father** will want to focus on his relationship with his daughter and possibly provide an anecdote or recollection about her as a child. He should also welcome the groom into his family with some reference to things that they have in common, and propose a toast to the newly-weds.

The **groom**'s role is to thank his father-in-law for the toast, for his daughter, for the wedding reception and for being welcomed into the family. Often he will include some romantic reference to when he first met his bride and maybe a humorous self-deprecating anecdote. He should also thank the guests for coming and for their gifts. It is customary to give presents to the best man, ushers, pageboys and bridesmaids at this stage, and to thank them for all their help. The groom proposes a toast to the bridesmaids.

I think that both the bride's father and the groom should aim to speak for a maximum of five minutes unless they are very accomplished and experienced speakers. The best man can allow himself longer, but not more than ten minutes including time for laughter.

You probably won't be a groom more than once or twice in your life but you may get more practice at being a **best man**. It is expected that he provides the humorous speech, but remember that your audience will be of many different ages and attitudes and beware of embarrassing either the groom or the bride in front of their closest relatives and friends. The best man thanks the groom and bride for their gifts on behalf of the bridesmaids, ushers and pageboys, and compliments them on a job well done. He can include a toast to absent friends, to the bride and groom's future happiness and to the host and hostess. He may also be expected to act as the master of ceremonies and explain what other activities are taking place after the meal, such as a disco or band for dancing. If you feel you need some hints on incorporating humour into your speech have a look at Chapter 13 on using humour.

Whatever the style of wedding at which you are speaking your guiding principle should be sincerity. Avoid the clichés and banalities and speak from the heart and you won't go far wrong.

Leaving Parties

The tone of the event will probably be set by the popularity of the 'leaver' and the length of their involvement or employment.

If you're the one saying goodbye to the leaver don't slag them off for departing. A journalist friend of mine who was leaving the *Guardian* was amused by the remark of his editor, whose first sentence in his farewell speech to his old employee was, 'Well, John's leaving us to join the *Observer*, a choice fewer people are making these days.' Remember to thank them for what they've done, even if they've been pretty useless. This is the time to be generous and to acknowledge their contribution. One manager who kept personnel records going back scores of years had a tradition of looking up the departing employee's application for the job and reading from his notes of the interview. As no one else had access to them he was able to exaggerate and improvise to everyone's great amusement.

If you're the one leaving don't try and settle old scores or slag off the organisation – you never know, you might want to go back there some day, or at the very least ask for a decent reference. There will probably be people who have been responsible for your progress through the organisation and this is your opportunity to thank them publicly for their support. You can also recall some of your cock-ups in the early days before you knew how to do your job. This is always amusing for people to hear, especially if you are now in a senior role.

Impromptu Speaking

> 'Impromptu speeches aren't worth the paper they're written on.' LORD GODDARD

One of Winston Churchill's critics said, 'Winston has spent the best years of his life preparing his impromptu speeches.' It was actually a compliment; clever speakers are always prepared.

In fact you can often anticipate when you might be expected to 'say a few words'. Before any meeting, study the agenda as it might suggest the topics on which you could be asked to comment. Informal meetings or leaving parties may not schedule a speaker, but you could anticipate whether you would be the best person to make a toast or offer a few words of thanks.

Good impromptu speeches are prepared with as much care as any others and delivered so skilfully that they appear effortless. A true impromptu speech arises with no preparation time, so if the situation might occur, plan how you would respond. Remember that every day of your life you are speaking without preparation so you know you have the ability to do so. Don't allow self-consciousness to hamper your self-expression. Some speakers collect short quotes or anecdotes they can deliver on the spur of the moment and that are appropriate for semi-formal occasions.

If you are asked to speak unexpectedly you can use one or two of the following techniques:

- Pause thoughtfully, admit you have not prepared, but don't apologise. Agree with the other speakers – and decline to comment further.

- Build on the earlier speaker's comments or summarise what has been said previously. This is probably the easiest way to start.

- Use mental prompts – why? how? which? when? what? who? – to build up your response.

- Tell an anecdote – this is particularly effective if it is personal or humorous, but it must be relevant to the topic of the meeting or gathering.

- Pick a structure, e.g. past, present, future; problem/solution.

- Restate the problem and add your own views.

- End with a quote, e.g. 'I know that you believe you have understood what you think I said, but I am not sure you realise that what you heard is not what I meant.'

Introducing a Speaker

Introductions should always be short; after all, the audience is there to hear the speaker not you. Ask for details of the speaker's background in advance so that you have the authentic facts and not something gleaned from dubious sources. Unfortunately, what you are given may be something that looks good when used as a biography in a book but doesn't sound right when you are speaking it. You will need to edit the details you've been given so that that you can give the speaker's credentials without making them sound like his CV. I also like to find out some personal details such as those about family, the type of house he lives in and where he goes on holiday. Your introduction might go something like this: 'So when Jim is not researching the structure of DNA he lives in a cottage in Oxfordshire with his wife, two teenage sons and a Labrador called Spot. He has just come back from hiking the Inca Trail in Peru.'

Vote of Thanks

You may be called upon to give a vote of thanks to a speaker or to someone who has provided a specific service to your group. To some degree both of these can be prepared in advance. If you know the topic about which the speaker will be talking you can research it. Make notes during his talk and refer in brief to the main items of interest to you. With any vote of thanks it's important to make what you say sound sincere and personal – avoid clichés such as 'We are all so grateful …' Try to identify the unique contribution that has been made by the person and the effect it has had on you and your group.

How to Run Effective Meetings

Before you decide to hold a meeting, ask yourself why you want to hold it and what would happen if you didn't. If you cannot come up with satisfactory answers don't have the meeting.

If you go ahead, you need to consider these points:

- What type of meeting is needed? For example, do you need the meeting to give or get information, or to decide or persuade?

- How should it be structured?

- Who should attend?

- Does everyone need to be there for the whole time?

- Who should chair the meeting?

- What problems might arise at it?

- When and where should it be held?

- How long should it last?

Informing people

Even for an informal meeting, adequate notice is essential. However, just a memo with date, time and place is insufficient. People must be aware of the subject of the meeting, its purpose and the kind of information they may be expected to provide. Telling people what is expected of them only when they turn up is time-wasting and annoying. It often results in circular and repetitive discussion and in decisions being made based on faulty or inadequate information.

Consulting people

You can anticipate many of the problems that occur at meetings by talking in advance to the people who will be present. If you are forewarned about a problem, you have a much greater chance of solving it before the meeting, or of dealing with it effectively. If the purpose of the meeting is to report on progress, those who haven't made any progress (often through no fault of their own) may be very defensive and try to cover this up. Talk through the problems with them before the meeting and see if you can move on to something positive – for example possible solutions to the problem.

Hidden agendas

A hidden agenda is when someone does something for an undeclared, and often deliberately concealed reason. For example, they may question you about a situation, apparently in order to get more information. However, their real motive may be to undermine your position by proving they know more about the situation than you do. Hidden agendas are usually difficult to detect, and may only surface gradually during a discussion. If you can identify them at an early stage, or are at the very least prepared for them, you have a much greater chance of dealing with them.

Who should attend?

The ideal number of people at a meeting depends on the aim of the meeting. For example, if the aim is simply to inform, a relatively large number of people can be present. If the purpose is to find solutions to shared problems, the success of the meeting can be seriously threatened if there are too many people present. Four to seven people is ideal; ten is tolerable; twelve is the limit. Invite people for what they may be expected to contribute rather than for what they may need to know.

Who should take the chair?

Chairing a meeting can be very demanding. Probably the most difficult type of meeting is the one where you hope to reach a group decision through consensus: it is almost impossible to chair this type of meeting effectively unless you manage to remain uninvolved and impartial. If you have very strong views on a subject you'll almost certainly steer the discussion in a specific direction, encourage those who agree with you and cut off those who disagree. You may well do these things unconsciously – but you will do them!

If, therefore, you are very involved and hold strong views, yet want to encourage genuine consensus, get someone who is impartial to take the chair. It may be that this will only apply to one or two agenda items, so stand down for them. There is no rule that says the same person must be in the chair for the whole meeting.

Chairing skills

If you are the chair, your main tasks are to ensure that everyone who should contribute does so, and to prevent any one person (including yourself) from dominating. Remember to ask for facts to support opinions and make sure meanings are clear for everyone. People will expect you to recognise and summarise the agreements and disagreements but keep the discussion to the point and moving forwards. It is important to recognise when to bring each agenda item to a close in order to achieve the objective of the meeting. As the chair you have several tools at your disposal: listening and observing, asking questions and summarising.

If you are simply attending the meeting you sometimes also need to think about all these tasks – especially if they are not being done by the chair.

How to get started

Always start a meeting on time. If you wait for latecomers to arrive it'll encourage them to be late again. In addition, the people who arrived on time the first time will be late too, as they know the meeting won't start punctually. If necessary carry out any introductions and remember that it's particularly important that the person taking the minutes knows who everyone is. Restate the aim and the limits of the meeting. For example: 'We're here to decide how to implement the new system. We are not here to discuss the type of system we need – that has already been decided.'

Sometimes it's good to summarise the situation that has led to the meeting and define any necessary terms. It is amazing how long people can argue without realising that they're talking about different things. Confirm the structure of the meeting and remind people of the time constraints. If you establish ground rules at the start ('I want to hear from everyone, but bear in mind that there are tight time constraints.') it's much easier for you to enforce them as you go through. Try to prevent people from interrupting – but do come back to them. Let the persistent interrupters have their say at an appropriate time, and then make it clear to them that you want to hear other people's views. Without stifling creative thought, don't allow the discussion to wander from the point and don't allow sub-meetings – if these occur ask the people involved to share what they are saying with the rest of the group. Try and control the very talkative by asking closed, factual questions. Remember the power of body language in communication and show that you're listening to everyone and taking them seriously.

You must be absolutely clear about what you want to achieve by the end of your meeting. Simply saying, 'We need to have a meeting to talk about XYZ' is guaranteed to lead to a lot of wasted time and effort.

You may have different objectives for different parts of the meeting (but beware of trying to achieve too much at once).

Here are some of the possible objectives.

- To reach decisions as a body.

- To help someone make a decision.

- To decide how to implement a decision.

- To give information.

- To get information.

- To pool information.

- To brainstorm.

- To allow grievances to be aired.

If your objective involves making a decision, what exactly are you trying to decide?

Encouraging discussion

Not everyone needs to contribute to every agenda item – so if someone is silent, think about possible reasons before inviting them to speak. If you know someone is shy or more junior, yet has something valuable to contribute, tell them in advance you'll be asking their opinion on the specific topic. Lead into their contribution gently. For example, say, 'Bob, I know you've had a lot of experience with XYZ and have done some research into how it could affect us. Can you tell us about it?' Use open questions, for example, 'Sue, how will that affect your team?' or 'John, what do you think about that?' You might find that shy people prefer to talk about facts than about opinions.

Ending the meeting

As chair it's your job to bring the meeting to an end, or to have a break, when you've achieved your objective, or when it's obvious you can't achieve it because more information is needed or the right people aren't present. Sometimes you have to finish a meeting if it becomes clear that people need more time to think, or if feelings are running so high that logical discussion becomes impossible. Alternatively, people may have become tired and stale and are no longer thinking creatively so you must call a halt. Finally, if you've run out of time you have to finish. At the end of the meeting, summarise where you have got to, what's been decided and what's to happen next.

Writing the minutes

There are two types of minutes: decisions only (who is to do what by when), and decisions with a summary of the main arguments leading up to the decision. All minutes should include:

- Time, date and venue of meeting; who it was chaired by.

- Names of those present, apologies for absence, who was present for some items and who arrived late.

- All agenda items discussed and decisions reached. If action was agreed, record who has to do what by when.

- Date, time and place of next meeting (if appropriate).

The best way to create accurate minutes is to agree during the meeting what is to go in them. Ideally the chairperson should sum up at the end of each agenda point and get agreement on what should be minuted. If you're taking the minutes and aren't clear what has been decided, ask then and there.

When writing the minutes, remember that you're providing a factual record of the meeting and that your style of writing should reflect this. Keep your sentences short, your words simple, your style direct and to the point, and your meaning clear.

Contributors' rights and responsibilities

If you are attending a meeting you have certain rights and responsibilities – for instance, stating your opinion and putting forward suggestions and making your contributions without being interrupted by others; having your opinions and suggestions listened to and reacted to, as well as disagreeing with views and suggestions put forward by others.

As a contributor, you must control your own behaviour so that it helps rather than hinders the progress of the meeting. You also have responsibilities such as keeping your contribution short, avoiding interrupting others and not letting them interrupt you, making your contributions at the right time and helping to improve the effectiveness of the meeting.

SUMMARY

- Never allow yourself to be forced into speaking – someone else might be better and less emotionally involved.

- Identify why you are speaking and consider the needs of the whole audience. Avoid embarrassing anyone present.

- Prepare in advance even if it is an impromptu talk.

- Chairing skills can be learnt and are essential to achieve outcomes without wasting time.

5

Holding Your Audience's Attention

'Speak properly and in as few words as you can,
but always plainly, for the end of speech is not ostentation,
but to be understood.'
WILLIAM PENN

Before I suggest some ideas on how to hold your audience's attention, let's revisit the main differences between reading and listening, which are important if you are going to be able to write and deliver a convincing and natural presentation.

I have already described the problems of keeping the attention of your listeners with the spoken word (see page 3). *Listening is not easy.* The listener's thoughts provide a plethora of distractions. Reading is different; a reader who is distracted rereads a sentence or paragraph or even an entire chapter. On the first day of a holiday have you had the experience of repeatedly rereading the opening of your book? You couldn't concentrate because your thoughts kept returning to the work you had left behind and the possible problems at home that might occur during your absence. However, if your mind wandered, you could return to your book and attempt to concentrate again. Listeners can't do this. If they don't concentrate during your talk, they don't have an opportunity of relistening. They only have *one chance to understand* what you are saying.

Readers can vary the speed of their reading and, if the material is complex or unfamiliar, they can stop and refer to a dictionary or even discuss it with a colleague. Listeners *can't vary the pace* of the speaker's delivery.

Readers can skim-read in order to see the total idea and reread what they feel is relevant. Listeners *can't anticipate your total talk*; only you know the complete picture, and therefore what might seem clear to you may be incomprehensible to your listeners.

Bearing in mind that listeners can't move backwards or forwards, or vary the speed of their listening, what can you do to help them to follow, understand and retain what you are saying?

Tell Them What to Expect

If you give your listeners an outline of your talk or a map to show them where you intend leading them, they will find it easier to follow you. This is the equivalent of the reader who skim-reads to identify the main points before settling down to read the detail. Here is how one speaker identified the path along which she was taking her listeners: 'There are three main areas that the marketing department has examined over the past six months. These are advertising, pricing and sales. During my talk, I am going to look at each of these in turn. Firstly, advertising ...' Even in a vote of thanks you can explain what you are going to cover. 'There are four people who deserve a special thank you. The first is Tom...'

Tell Them Where You Are

You can also help your listeners by summarising and recapping so that they know how far along the path you have progressed. Here is an example from the same speech: 'So, to summarise our two main recommendations on advertising, we recommend (a) more consumer advertising and (b) limited but clearly defined trade advertising. So much for our recommendations for the first area that we looked at – advertising. [pause] Now I'd like to turn to the second area – pricing.' You'll notice from this example that the speaker has numbered each of her points. In a vote of thanks you could say, 'I said I wanted to thank three people and I've mentioned Tom, Dick and Harry. The fourth is a surprise.'

In her final summary, the above speaker looked back and told the listeners what they had heard – this is the equivalent of the reader rereading to ensure he has understood: 'So the three areas the marketing department examined were advertising, pricing and sales and we are making the following three recommendations. Firstly, for advertising, we recommend more consumer advertising and limited but clearly defined advertisements for the trade. Second, on pricing, we recommend a new and simplified discount structure and, finally, on sales, we recommend a two-tier sales force. So a big thank you to Tom, Dick, Harry and Bob the Builder.'

In the written form, these recaps and summaries appear repetitious and even unnecessary, but remember they are not for the eye, but for the ear. Listeners need these reinforcements to help them follow you as well as to help them retain what you are saying; without them, it is like trying to read a book with no paragraphs or chapters.

Gather Up Your Stragglers

You know that listeners are not concentrating consistently so you must gather them up as you progress along your path. *Rhetorical questions* are excellent for attracting listeners back from their mental undergrowth. You might ask, 'So how do these new plans affect you in the sales department?' or in a wedding speech, 'So what possible reason could there have been to ask me to be best man?'

Listeners will concentrate on your answer because you have involved them with a rhetorical question and you have also indicated what is coming next. Use rhetorical questions throughout your script – they are powerful attention grabbers and signposts to what is to follow.

You can also *anticipate your audience's reaction* by saying, 'You may be asking yourself what on earth this has got to do with the sales department, or wondering how Sally met Harry in the first place.'

With this technique, you are anticipating that your listeners are about to wander off your path into their mental undergrowth and are enticing them back before they can stray too far.

Remember to *recap constantly*, particularly in a business presentation, as you progress from one point to another; this will help people who have disappeared down Route 350 and may have lost the thread of your argument. Their own thoughts are continually interrupting their concentration and you need to help them follow the logic of your talk by signposting each point and recapping frequently. One speaker, who was presenting a problem/solution structure to her staff group, used a combination of recapping and rhetorical questions to help her audience follow her talk: 'I told you I would be tackling the problem of our lack of expansion from two angles: the shortage of available funds and overstocking of merchandise. First, I've given you the details of our current financial situation. You may be wondering what these figures really mean. I can best answer that by referring to my second point – overstocking. Why have we got a warehouse full of navy blue suits? Let me tell you ...'

In this example the speaker has reminded the audience that she will be tackling the problem from two angles; she tells them that she has already given details of the first point, raises their awareness of what she is talking about with a rhetorical question and announces the second point she is going to discuss.

Appeal to the Emotions

Facts and information on their own won't change anyone's mind. You must show *why* your ideas will benefit the listeners. This is where probing questions asked in advance of your meeting pay off. You know what sort of people you are facing. You have assessed what makes them tick. Simply convert your facts into advantages for them. Demonstrate how your solution can solve their problem. Explain how you can cater for their needs. Be sure to describe advantages that are relevant to *them*.

Here are a few examples of facts followed by advantages:

- This is a book on effective speaking (fact). Reading it will help you to present your ideas in a convincing manner (advantage).

- It is a short book (fact). Therefore it's easy to carry and you can read it anywhere (advantage).

- It is reasonably priced (fact). You can become a more effective speaker than your colleagues for a small outlay (advantage).

Another interesting example of facts and advantages or features and benefits was described in the following way by a DIY tool salesman: 'I don't sell the drill, I sell the holes.' You don't buy a drill because it has the most impressive features, you buy it because of its ability to make holes, i.e. what it can do for you.

In order to convert facts or information into an advantage for your listeners, you must ask yourself what these facts or information will do for them. What benefit will this provide? What need will this satisfy? Your listeners will not buy ideas unless they recognise that they have a problem your ideas will solve. Once they have seen the need, however, they will be more receptive to the advantages and benefits of your ideas, provided they satisfy that need. They may be uninterested in the facts and only interested in the advantages that they provide. You may choose to begin by showing the benefits that appeal to their emotions and follow them with a logical description of the facts. Changes of attitude and decision making can depend as much on an emotional response as on rational arguments.

Make It Easy for Them to Agree

Don't expect to convert your listeners to your views instantly. No one likes to admit that they are wrong, so make it easy for them. Encourage them to contribute by allowing them to acknowledge some of the benefits. Persuasion is often achieved by letting the listeners talk themselves into accepting your point of view. Sometimes you can smooth the path for them by revealing that you used to share their point of view. You can tell them how a particular advantage convinced you to change your mind. In this way they keep their self-esteem while agreeing with you. Your aim is to persuade your listeners to adopt your ideas, without causing them to feel that they are 'wrong' and that you are 'right'.

With practice, you will be able to convince listeners that your solution was really theirs. Coaches and mentors learn the art of non-judgemental listening until their clients work out their own problems. You may need to push and prod a listener towards your selected goal, but it's surprising how often people will adopt new ideas with little resistance, providing they feel that they haven't been forced into it – steer clear of the hard sell.

Ask for Commitment

Make sure that your listeners are committed to your ideas and that, if necessary, an agreement is reached on the action that should follow, for example: 'So we are agreed that we'll keep the front office open between Christmas and the New Year but the factory will be closed during that period. How shall we announce this decision?' or 'So we are agreed that an extra £100 will be added to the tenants' service charges to cover cleaning of the stairwell.' Once a commitment has been made, steer clear of any further discussion and refrain from looking triumphant.

A Convincing Delivery

To convince and persuade successfully you must have personal commitment. You must believe in your cause and be able to show that you do. A nonchalant, unemotional presentation will fail. You must be able to *show enthusiasm*. It's not enough to feel it, you must display your heart on your face and in your voice. You can't simply read out notes or, even worse, a script and hope to express heartfelt emotion. Your emotions should be part of you. Reading a script under these circumstances suggests that you are not being honest. You need eye contact to demonstrate sincerity. Remember that the impact of your words will be diminished by poor body language. In fact, if your words say one thing and your body another, you run the risk of appearing hypocritical and deceitful.

Don't allow yourself to be interrupted or distracted by comments from other members of the group. Don't allow your voice to drop at the end of each sentence. Make sure you have sufficient breath in your lungs to carry your voice to the end.

Try to match your body language to that of your audience. Students of body language have discovered that people who feel at ease with each other tend, unconsciously, to sit or stand in a similar fashion and to change their positions to match each other. You can observe this in restaurants, in public lounges and even at office meetings. Those who are in agreement will be sitting in a similar manner. The dissenter will be leaning backwards or forwards to demonstrate his disagreement physically. We naturally follow this 'mirroring' of those with whom we feel comfortable, without even being aware of it. To create a harmonious atmosphere for your persuasion, try to ensure that your body language doesn't conflict with that of your listeners. For example, if your listener is sitting and you are standing as you try to convince him that he should do extra homework over the weekend, your chances of success will be improved if you place yourself at his level. All your communication should be face to face. You are not seeking to intimidate or force your listeners to accept your views, so aim to balance your body language with theirs.

The adage that 'People buy people first' holds true. Often your listeners will not be assessing the value of your ideas. They will be judging *you*. If they like you, they'll want to believe in you and your opinions, even when they can find no logical reason for doing so. Appealing to people's emotions makes a lot of sense, provided that this doesn't result in them feeling manipulated.

Involving Techniques

However passionate a speaker you are, if you talk at your listeners continuously you won't convince or persuade them. They are likely to escape down Route 350. Remember, they may want to make a point, ask a question or even agree with you.

Schedule *pauses* into your presentation so that you can invite your listeners to contribute: 'Can you see how this new schedule would make revising for your exams less of a nightmare?' or 'How do you feel this could fit into your existing budget?' or 'How does this sound to you?'

Vary the words you use to appeal to your listeners' senses. Some people can '*feel* an idea', while others want to '*hear* how it sounds' or '*see* how it's going to work'. You can identify from their conversation which category of words is most comfortable for them.

How Else Can You Help the Audience to Listen?

Facts on their own tend to be dull and you will need to translate them into *visual word pictures*: 'Our warehouse handled twenty tons of merchandise this year. That's about equivalent to a row of eight terraced houses,' or 'Our hotel inspectors travelled over 80,000 miles each this year; that's like going to Manchester from London 400 times.'

Try to illustrate with *personal examples*. This speaker was describing the drawbacks of being self-employed: 'Many people envy me because I work from home, but you know I never get away from my "office" and I find myself opening business letters even on a Saturday morning.'

Nothing helps an audience understand as well as *personal stories*. I remember seeing a very successful headmistress graphically telling an audience about her first disastrous class and how she had gone home and nearly given up on the spot. It was her own story and all the audience shared her feelings of rejection and admired her determination to carry on.

The audience will always warm to you if you can reveal your own feelings and weaknesses. It can be difficult to do so. For this reason, the audience will respect your courage. Early on in my training career, I remember making a remark towards the end of a day's training to the effect that I had felt nervous at the start of the day. I was amazed at the number of people who were reassured by this comment and pleased that I was prepared to make it to them. On reflection I realised that it was because I had felt comfortable with the group that I was able to describe my feelings. If you build in a few *self-revealing sentences*, your audience will feel you are treating them as friends.

Use personal anecdotes to support your arguments. If you have experiences that illustrate your main point, the audience will understand and remember them more easily.

Use Relevant Illustrations

Make sure your anecdotes or examples are relevant to your audience. I once heard a successful talk to a group of school-boys by a management consultant, in which he compared management with being the captain of a cricket team, matching and balancing the strengths and personalities of the players. On another occasion a politician was discussing government revenue and expenditure in terms of billions of pounds; this could be difficult to comprehend for some people, until he equated it to the wages and bills that are familiar to every householder: 'Some bills have to be paid every week while others can be paid every month – but you have to make sure you save a bit every week to pay them.' The amounts may be larger but the principles are the same.

In a sales presentation, you may want to paint a word picture of how your customer will feel if she buys your product, by describing a similar situation with another customer: 'He told me he felt a great sense of relief after the new coffee machine was installed – no more rows about whose turn it was to make coffee.'

The majority of road accidents happen within five miles of the home: just another boring statistic until a doctor friend of mine told me that if he hadn't been wearing his seatbelt, he wouldn't be alive today. He had popped out to buy a newspaper and had had a bad accident.

I have heard a police superintendent, who appeared to be remote from the problems of his officers, vividly describing the times when he was 'on the beat' and had a boss who made impossible demands on him. His stories were relevant to the audience and illustrated many of the points in his talk.

Appealing to the Listener

If you want to be persuasive, put yourself in your listeners' shoes and ask yourself how you can help them to follow your talk and what will make it relevant to them.

Some speakers like to follow the FEB technique:

Feature or Fact
Effect of the F
Benefit to the listener

This technique is applied in the following way: 'Because [feature], you will be able to [effect] which means that [benefit].' For example, '*Because* we have expanded the car park, *you will always be able to* park, *which means that* you will save time whenever you come to the community centre.'

The words 'because', 'you will be able to' and 'which means that' are only intended as a guide and you can choose your own phrases to fit the sense of your sentence. Here's another example: 'As the council has accepted this proposal, you can start work immediately and say goodbye to your money problems.'

As you prepare your talk, imagine that you have to answer listeners who are asking, 'So what? What does this mean? How does this affect me, my organisation, my situation, my family?' You should be able to answer those questions with FEB.

Talking Numbers

In general, try to avoid speaking numbers as they are difficult to grasp by ear and can even be confusing. Unless precision is essential, round up figures so that the listeners will be able to identify them more easily – for example, say 'nearly half' instead of '48.27 per cent', or 'just over three-quarters' instead of '76.92 per cent'. You could work out a method of showing a measurement so that it means more to the audience: 'From earth to the moon is 240,250 miles. That's a long way, but how far is it really? Well, if you got into your car and drove every day for ten hours at fifty miles per hour, you would arrive there in sixteen months, which is on 11 May next year.'

Some talks are based on figures, so consider using a visual aid or handout to help your listeners to follow your reasoning more easily.

Size

Size is also difficult to visualise unless you compare it with a familiar object – for example, smaller than a matchbox; about the size of two double-decker buses; as high as that ceiling; as long as this room.

Avoid Jargon and Abbreviations

Beware of speaking in terms that are unfamiliar to your audience – this can be very distracting and can cause many of your listeners to switch their energy to ponder on the meaning of a phrase or abbreviation and so lose the thread of your argument.

Some terminology or abbreviations that are part of your everyday vocabulary when talking to colleagues could be misleading or even incomprehensible to many people outside your immediate circle. Carefully trim these distractions from your talk. Explain abbreviations at the beginning of your talk. If you feel you must use shorthand because the unabbreviated names are too long, remember to include the full name from time to time. Sometimes when listening to a radio interview I will hear the speaker using an abbreviation that is familiar to him but unclear to the listener. The interviewer will step in with an explanation: 'So DLR, that's the Docklands Light Railway isn't it?' As you don't have the benefit of someone to explain your jargon make sure that you edit your words carefully beforehand.

Convenient Clichés or Piquant Prose

This is an important point because speakers can often be unaware that they habitually use imprecise words and hackneyed phrases that are boring to the listener. Here is an example of what I mean:

> I'm absolutely delighted that so many of you could come here tonight as it's raining cats and dogs outside, but at least it's warm and snug in here. I've been asked to speak to you tonight and I don't mind telling you that I'm a bundle of nerves and I hope I haven't bitten off more than I can chew.
>
> I know I can depend on your support so I won't mince matters. Let's face it, things often get worse before they get better. So, not to put too fine a point on it, I'm going to ask you to stick it out. From the bottom of my heart, I appeal to you to put yourselves in my shoes at this point in time. Is this a fate worse than death? I can safely say I think it is, so without further ado, I'll leave you with this thought as I beat a hasty retreat, better safe than sorry, at the end of the day.

Of course no one would include so many clichés but it's often easier to use a familiar phrase than to find a more original expression. Try to avoid clichés that have ceased to have an impact – if you don't, your listeners will find you uninspiring and may eventually stop listening. It takes time to be creative and imaginative, but if you invest in a dictionary of synonyms you'll find that your speech will become livelier and more entertaining.

SUMMARY

- Remember to announce the structure, and share your route map with your listeners.

- Summarise and recap frequently to show how far you've travelled and where you've been.

- Identify each point clearly to indicate the landmarks of your journey.

- Use rhetorical questions to regain the audience's attention and point out the signposts.

- Use examples, personal stories and anecdotes that are relevant to the audience to illustrate your ideas as if you were describing the beauty spots of your journey.

- Avoid jargon and abbreviations – beware of using 'foreign' language.

- Summarise the main points and, if necessary, ask for action before you conclude, as if you were recalling the landmarks of your trip before arriving home.

6

Designing Effective Visual Aids

'Every picture tells a story.'
Advertising slogan for Sloane's backache and kidney pills, circa 1907

Visual aids, if properly used, can be effective for holding your listeners' attention. In this chapter I describe the advantages and disadvantages of the most commonly used visual aids, as well as how to design and make visuals that will enhance your talk or presentation. In the next chapter you will find hints on how to use visual aid equipment.

Adding Audience Value

The objective of many presentations is to inform or persuade, or a combination of both, but information received by listening is retained for less time than information that is received by seeing. This means that visual aids help to make your talk memorable. They also help to explain complex ideas in a form that is easily understood. Relationships and comparisons can be shown more clearly in a visual format, and statistics, figures and financial data in general are more digestible and comprehensible when presented visually.

Visuals can reinforce an idea that you have already discussed in words; for instance, you could outline a cost-saving theory and then show visually what the actual savings would be in practice.

Avoiding Aid Dependency

Speakers often regard visuals as the magic ingredient that will turn a turgid talk into a professional presentation. In fact I have seen more good talks ruined by inappropriate visuals than I have seen poor talks improved by good ones. Even when the visuals are good, the speaker often finds it difficult to incorporate them smoothly so that they, and the speaker's behaviour, only distract the audience. So make sure your visual is *an aid* and not a distraction, and make sure your aid is *visual.*

Beware of adding visuals to your presentation for the wrong reasons; they can take time, be difficult to use and confuse the audience. Many speakers I know use them as a prompt. They have most of their presentation on slides and refer to them throughout their talk. Such speakers are ignoring all the advantages of talking to a live audience and suffering all the disadvantages of reading. Your audience can be reminded of your key points after you have spoken to them, so use a visual to summarise but not as a prompt.

Don't use visuals to brighten up an uninteresting talk – improve your talk and only use a visual to illustrate it more vividly. Also don't be tempted to add visuals because the other speakers are doing so. Your talk may not need them. In some organisations, if you arrive at a meeting without visuals you are judged to be ill-prepared. It can be difficult to go against a strong corporate culture; however, you could reduce the number of visuals and improve your delivery so that people look and listen to *you.* Wean them and yourself off visual aid dependency. Instead use visuals to:

- present facts, concepts and figures in a comparative or structured form;

- aid comprehension and prevent misunderstanding;

- reinforce your message;

- focus your listeners' attention;

- maintain interest and help retention;

- motivate the audience to make a decision;

- add humour and spice.

Non-negotiable Visual Aids

There are some situations where visual aids are essential. The first is when you want to show an idea visually. On page 25 you will see a sketch of a mind map. This concept is also described in the text (see page 24), but I think you'll agree that seeing an example makes it is easier to understand. Any discussion about techniques or methods can benefit from a visual illustrating how they work in practice. Cut-away drawings of machinery or tools can be very helpful on practical, instructional courses. I have heard that you can always recognise an MBA graduate because they can't resist drawing business models! Nevertheless, this is another example of how a visual aid adds value to an idea.

Figures are difficult to understand when spoken. Comparisons can be made more easily when they are displayed visually. Here is a pie chart showing the relative importance of three factors to consider when speaking. These figures have already appeared in the book (see page 6), but I think you'll agree they make more impression when portrayed as shown in the illustration.

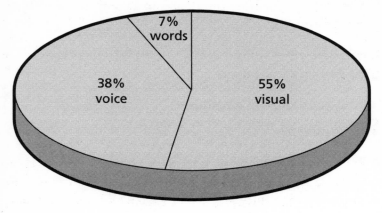

Speakers' impact

Considerations for Visual Aids

Once you have decided that your talk would benefit from the inclusion of some visual material, choosing how to display it can be difficult. The table (see page 80) shows the advantages and disadvantages of the various types of visual aid and you'll see that not one of them is perfect. However, here are some of the considerations for you to bear in mind when selecting a visual style.

Available equipment

Most companies have a data projector and flip chart, but if you are presenting a talk off site, check the specifications of the data projector. Audio-visual equipment is available to hire in most large cities, but if you are using hired equipment, don't try to save money by only ordering it for the day of your talk. Make sure you can rehearse with it in advance and, for more complex presentations with several speakers, ensure that you have it for one or even two days before the actual presentation. Hotel equipment varies from excellent to appalling, so ensure you see it beforehand in order to check its suitability for your talk. I have run courses throughout the UK and am amazed at how some hotels offering 'conference facilities' can be so unaware of what is needed by speakers.

Size of audience

If the audience can't see what's on the visual, you are likely to antagonise them and lose their attention. Certain aids – for example flip chart, blackboard and whiteboard – aren't suitable for groups of more than twenty-five people. This is a rough estimate, and the size and layout of the room may allow you to increase or decrease that number. If you are presenting to a small group of five or six people, don't dismiss the idea of visuals as inappropriate; a large screen is not always necessary as you can easily project on to a blank wall.

Size and layout of room

Long, narrow rooms with poor lighting are not suitable for the smaller aids such as flip charts. Sometimes conference facilities offered by older hotels are located in rooms with pillars or asymmetric walls that can make it difficult to set up a screen which is visible to all the audience. If you are sitting on a platform you may have to rearrange the speakers' chairs so that they don't obstruct the screen.

Lighting

You may have to darken the room. Some offices don't have blinds at the windows and I have come across hotel rooms with curtains that are decorative but not functional. You rarely see overhead projectors these days, but the slides can be shown in natural light, although you will occasionally need to block out sunlight if it is shining directly on to the screen. Also, low-power data projectors need dimmed lights. Avoid shadows on the flip chart if possible and don't place it against a window or any other source of bright light as this will make it difficult to read.

Seating arrangements

Make sure you arrange the seating so that everyone has a clear view of the screen. In the seating diagrams (see pages 228–9) you will see that the position of the projector and screen can usually be adjusted so that it's visible to everyone.

Cost versus frequency of use

Slides can be made easily in the office, but for sales presentations to clients or large conferences, consider using a design company. If you are using the slides repeatedly, for instance if you are part of a road show travelling around the country, or if you are utilising them for training and teaching purposes, it's worth the extra expense to have them professionally designed and produced.

Visual aids

Advantages	*Disadvantages*
Laptops/Data Projectors	
Have all the advantages of overhead projector and 35mm slides; available to most presenters; smooth transitions between slides;	Maximum of two people can see laptop screen so usually a data projector is required; extended set-up time and technical failure

Advantages	Disadvantages
look professional; use of special effects and sound adds impact and interest; enable you to check slide by looking at your laptop, not over your shoulder to screen.	can reflect badly on presenter; presenter can be tied to laptop unless remote control is used; colour on laptop may change when projected.

Video Clips

Can be incorporated into laptop presentation or played on monitors; add movement and external presenters.	Sound reproduction on laptop can be of low quality so use external speakers; use sparingly or the video will dominate your presentation.

Flip Chart

Easy to use; not much can go wrong; readily available; cheap; versatile – can be used pre-written or constructed during course of talk; portable.	Can be difficult to write on quickly; only suitable for small audience of less than twenty people.

Whiteboards

Similar advantages to blackboards but less messy; also presentation clearer with special pens; easy and clean to use.	Limited to small groups; generally only available in training rooms; not portable.

Physical Objects

Can save unnecessary description; ensure everyone has uniform idea of what speaker is talking about; members of audience can handle them – direct contact is always useful; versatile; objects and props often easily available.	Passing round objects is time-consuming and distracting; small groups only, holding up article unsuitable for small objects or large audiences; models can be expensive to prepare.

Blackboards

No mechanisms to go wrong; flexible; mistakes easily corrected; can be quickly erased.	Chalk is messy to use; creates a classroom atmosphere; difficult to erase well if old; suitable for small groups only; not portable.

Advantages	*Disadvantages*
Overhead Projectors	
Transparencies easily and economically produced on PowerPoint; screen is bright and clear in normal room light; suitable for small or large audiences; can be used like flip chart with a continuous roll of acetate so that speaker can write calculations or notes on to it.	Rarely used these days so can appear old-fashioned; can break down or suffer bulb failure; usually fan cooled so produce background noise that can be distracting; must be constantly switched on and off so as not to leave irrelevant material or a blank screen showing.
35mm Slides	
Very sharp, bright image; focus attention of audience; wide variety of material can be shown; easily stored and carried; readily available; suit any size audience; useful for formal method of presentation.	Largely replaced by data projectors. Low light makes it difficult for audience to make notes and for speaker to maintain eye contact; less flexible than overhead projector; cannot change order or omit slides; artwork can be expensive.

How to Design Effective Visuals

Most of what I include in this section applies to slides that are produced on the Microsoft software programme PowerPoint. However, some of the basic rules regarding simplicity and clarity are also applicable to prepared flip charts. Even if you have an in-house audio visual department or if you intend to use an outside agency, as a speaker, you should have a good idea of what makes a successful visual, as they will need to follow your instructions.

Avoid verbal visuals

As we know, a picture is worth a thousand words. Unfortunately, in many of the presentations I see, a thousand words have been put on the visual aids.

Words rarely make good visuals, but many speakers consider that their listeners will be unable to follow a talk without a script in front of them. The greatest insult of all is to start your presentation with a visual proclaiming 'Good Morning' or 'Sales Presentation for . . .' Words on a visual encourage your listeners to become readers and while they are readers, they can't be listeners.

Verbal visuals can be a distraction as members of your audience will be reading at different speeds and if you attempt to read the slide for them, most of them will have finished before you anyway.

Bullet point slides are best limited to five words per point and five points per slide. You can omit a number at the beginning of each point and a full stop at the end of it. The points should be brief and punchy phrases, not full sentences, or even, perish the thought, paragraphs. The only exception I would make to this recommendation is when you are talking to overseas audiences whose knowledge of English may be variable. In this case, word slides can help them follow your presentation more easily. This is particularly true of Japanese audiences. For more on this, see page 298.

Remember that word slides can be made more interesting by using text shadow, backgrounds and shapes. Reveal your bullet points one by one by using PowerPoint transitions and build-up slides (see also page 85).

Any words included on your visuals must be legible from the seats furthest from the screen. Use a uniform typeface, and upper and lower case throughout, and always write words horizontally, even in pie charts or when identifying equipment parts that may be positioned at an angle. Add bold or italics to highlight key words.

It is a simple matter to add pictures to your visuals by using a scanner or digital camera.

Keep them simple

PowerPoint offers a wealth of special effects and it's tempting to use all those fancy borders and elaborate templates. Try to resist the temptation. Instead, choose the simple background that will enhance, not obscure, your message, and avoid adding logos and slide headings that significantly reduce the usable area of your visual. Many visuals are ineffective because they are complicated and contain too much information. They are difficult to understand and therefore become a distraction. You may need to separate out material in order to present it on several slides, so analyse what is the most significant data and reject the rest. Remember, white space is your friend.

Bear in mind that round figures are easier to understand than exact ones – for instance, £1 million is more comprehensible than £1,103,284.83. If you are preparing a series of slides showing the information in stages, you could, for example, start with a graph showing the sales targets and add the actual sales figures; with the build-up technique you can add information to each slide; for instance, a map of Great Britain could be filled in with regional sales figures. This method allows you to remain in control of the speed at which your audience assimilates information and also to explain any inconsistencies or anomalies in the data. For example, a sales manager might say, 'You will notice that sales figures for Scotland appear to have increased at a faster rate than those for the rest of the country, but bear in mind that International Mechanics, one of our larger customers, moved to Aberdeen in January, so their sales are included in Scotland now.'

Tables of figures rarely make good visuals, as they often contain too much information and are difficult to read. Pie charts and bar charts are simpler devices for relaying that kind of data.

Keep them uniform

I have found that clients who once upon a time considered a few typed notes on an overhead projector slide to be an adequate visual aid will now sometimes go to the opposite extreme: after some tuition on the merits of creative visuals they will use the flip chart extensively, in between showing a PowerPoint slide show, with video and sound effects. Avoid using too many types of visual aid or attempting to make them too diverse. A jumble of typefaces and styles and a mixture of colours gives the impression that both speaker and company are disorganised and confused. Choose a clear, simple font like Arial or a classic font like Times New Roman, and a type size no smaller than 28 points, and use it throughout your slides with a bold background colour to create a smart effect. Maintain a consistent style throughout for borders, headings and company logo position. If you are using transitions (see below), ensure they are uniform and only use the special effects sparingly for impact.

Transitions and builds

Transitions and builds are the movement from one slide to the next, or the build-up of text or images on to or away from the visual aid.

Because they are available it is tempting to experiment with all of them. Your selection should reflect the overall atmosphere and key messages you wish to put across. For informal presentations, such as internal department meetings or training sessions, use two or three of the following transitions: fly from left, wipe right, box in and out, blinds and chequerboard.

For more formal audiences, such as clients, senior executives and shareholders, you could also use fly from left and wipe right as a safe transition, as well as dissolve between messages. Use cuts to highlight sub-messages. Add boxes in and out to vary your transitions.

For a more upbeat audience such as a sales conference, all the above are suitable, plus a fade through black to provide a complete change of scene. Flying points in from the top is also effective. For special interest use the split vertical out (curtain opening) to open and split vertical in (curtain closing) to end.

I recently saw a key message being pulled in by a sports car which stopped with a squeal of brakes. As this was the only 'special effect' in an otherwise serious presentation, it had impact. But I did notice that the discussion after the presentation seemed to centre on 'How did he do that trick with the car?' rather than the key message! This is always a danger with unusual effects.

Use Visual metaphors

Beware of using Clip Art; it is generally considered to be hackneyed and it seldom adds real value to the visual. However, you can find excellent pictures from the many photo libraries that exist for just this purpose. Here are two examples of visual metaphors that illustrated key points in an imaginative way.

The first was used by an applicant for a major position at a university. He wanted to illustrate that his management style was 'hands on', so throughout his presentation he showed a picture of a pair of hands (his own, which he had photographed earlier). He won the job against strong competition because, as they told him later, they liked and remembered his hands.

The other visual metaphor, which was employed by a pharmaceutical company to illustrate how one of their medications for constipation should be displayed in a supermarket, was very simple and used a series of photos of plates. They began by asking 'How do people react to constipation?' The first slide showed an empty white plate with the words '22% do nothing', the next slide showed a plate with a packet of All Bran and the words '35% modify their diet', next they showed a plate with a pill and '16% take a laxative', and the last showed a plate with a pill and All Bran and '27% take both'. They had made their point that positioning laxatives alongside the All Bran would increase sales.

Keep them colourful

Judicial use of colour can significantly enhance your visuals, as you can use it as a background or to highlight important data, to underline and for bullet points and arrows. Aim for a contrast, for instance light letters on a dark background. If you are not confident about your colour sense use a colour wheel to guide you as to which colours complement each other.

If you want vibrant colours use the ones from opposite sides of the colour wheel (see page 88), for example orange and blue or yellow and purple. An image stands out strongly when a warm colour is combined with a cool colour. A common example of this is yellow lettering on a blue background.

However, some colours change or lose their intensity when they are projected. Always avoid white letters on a yellow background or vice versa, and pink on red, as they become invisible. You can use a different primary background colour or a different secondary colour as a side band to indicate the various sections of your talk – for example, the sales manager could use blue on the slides when illustrating her section on key accounts, and change to red when she moved on to new business. Avoid combinations of green and red, as these will be indistinguishable to people who are colour-blind. The key to using colour successfully is to keep it simple.

Keep them humorous

If you can introduce an element of humour into a serious presentation, you will be revealing the fun side of your

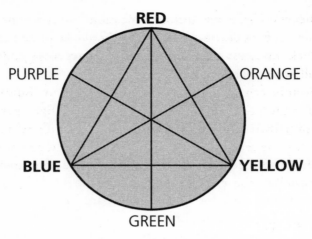

The colour wheel

character and this will warm your audience to you. Beware of being flippant, but you can add a light touch to dry material to help maintain your listeners' interest. For example, bar charts can depict your product. If you sell cars show your sales as bars shaped like vehicles.

Make your actual bullet point more interesting. Replace the standard dot or square with a symbol such as a pointing finger, a star or a representation of your key message, for example £££ or $$$ for increased revenue. Refer to the font options in PowerPoint under Wingdings for ideas.

Don't forget to double-check all visuals for typos and spelling mistakes *before* you show them to an audience.

Visual styles

Pie charts

A pie chart is a circle divided into 'slices', which visually indicates the relative value of each slice to the whole (see illustration, page 78). It is a very useful type of visual as it's easy to produce and suitable for both technical and non-technical audiences. Use as few sectors as possible and never exceed five or six. The most important sector should be placed at the 12 o'clock position and the other components arranged from the smallest to the largest or vice versa.

Sectors can be coloured or highlighted to indicate their importance, but be sure that any lettering or figures will show up over the background colour. Sometimes it's preferable to identify the sectors by means of arrows positioned at the side of the pie. Remember always to place your words horizontally; don't follow the shape of the pie.

Bar charts

Pie charts are useful in comparing fractions within a single whole, but bar charts can be used to highlight the relationship between two variables, for example age and salary, or productivity in geographical areas, as well as to illustrate trends and make comparisons. They should be simple and easy to follow, so when designing them, you must identify the relevant information and discard the rest, or present it as a second or third visual.

Bar charts can be drawn vertically or horizontally. The former are more appropriate for indicating a time element and when one item has to be shown several times, for example annual sales figures for the last five years. The timescale is normally shown along the bottom line.

Horizontal bar charts have two advantages: firstly, the information can be presented in any sequence, for instance sales figures for the month of July can be shown alphabetically by the rep's name, or by geographical area, or in order of size, or even randomly; secondly, there is more space to identify each bar. Remember that the labels can be placed at either end of each bar or even below and above it.

Sliding bar charts are used to show a sub-division within a total; for example, each bar showing sales figures could be sub-divided into sales for existing customers and sales from new customers. Using different colours for each division gives them more impact.

Line charts and graphs

These can be used instead of vertical bar charts and are particularly useful when a greater number of time periods needs to be illustrated; for instance, a three-year sales period with monthly totals would require thirty-six bars, which would be difficult to represent clearly. Line charts or graphs are also useful for illustrating minor variations in data, which would not be noticeable with bar charts. Variations can be highlighted by using a broken scale that does not begin at zero, but with the amount where the minor variation appears; for example, if the monthly sales figures over a twelve-month period ranged between £140,000 and £145,000 per month, the scale ranges from £135,000 to £155,000 in order to emphasise the variations. Be sure that the broken scale is clearly marked, otherwise the audience will assume that it starts at zero.

Flow and organisation charts

Flow charts illustrate the stages of development in a process or the passage of documents through a system, and organisation charts show the functional relationships and flow within a group or company. Both are useful to demonstrate visually links and connections that might be difficult to understand and remember without a chart (see page 77).

They can also be used to demonstrate visually the structure of your talk. Throughout your presentation, you can refer back to the organisation chart as a reminder to the audience of the structure and progress of your key points.

Tables of figures

These should be interpreted in a visual manner. However, if due to budgeting or time constraints this isn't possible, consider highlighting the key figures, so that the audience concentrates on them immediately and doesn't get drawn into reading the rest of the table. Block out the irrelevant information if you can. Remember that the figures on their own are insignificant without analysis, so don't leave the audience to puzzle over their meaning. Don't use the following on your visual:

- computer printouts;

- spread sheet material;

- detailed tables of figures;

- complex forms;

- printed material from books, newspapers or articles unless it is blown up to be legible or used only as montage.

Financial and technical presentations often suffer from too much detail. This is particularly noticeable when expert speakers are addressing lay audiences. If you are in this position, make sure that your audience research is thorough, enabling you to put yourself in their shoes. Stand back and isolate the most important features, and ignore the qualifying elements that may be fascinating to you because you are so closely involved with the subject. Aim to make your visuals simple and uncluttered by detail; show the audience the benefits to them of your argument, not the technical background.

Be Original

So far, this chapter has been devoted to the traditional methods of adding a visual element to your talk. But don't limit yourself. Be original. I saw a stimulating use of some very ordinary

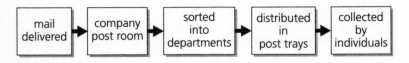

A flow chart showing the progress of mail through an office

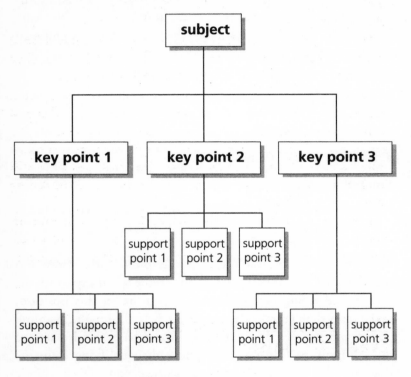

Organisational chart

props by a chairman during a presentation to his staff on the company's gross profit. He opened with: '£20 million sounds a lot of money, but what happens to it?' He proceeded to take a jug of orange juice and pour it into a number of glasses that he had set up on the table. 'So much has to go on wages and salaries,' he said, filling up one glass. 'We must allow this much for National Insurance Contributions and PAYE,' he said, as he moved on to the next glass. He proceeded to fill the rest of the glasses (he had marked the correct level for each one before he began his talk) with the overheads of the company. Eventually, he was left with a small amount of orange juice in the jug. 'This is what's left,' he said and measured it into the remaining two glasses. 'Just enough to pay Corporation Tax and dividends to the shareholders.' He held up the empty jug. 'So much for our profit.'

He had explained the financial situation to a non-financial audience in a manner that was easy to understand. Try to find new and simple methods of explaining complex material.

In this chapter I have not covered multimedia-supported presentations. However, if you wish to incorporate video and sound, ensure your clips are no longer than twenty seconds. To get an insight into how multimedia can be used most successfully, watch TV news programmes. You will see how still images are interwoven with video, and how sound, including music and sound effects, can add emphasis.

I believe the Internet is also having a strong influence on design, as well as providing a wealth of material for visual aids. Visit www.clearlypresented.com or www.presentersonline.com for inspiration.

Hints on Using a Production Company/ Events Organiser

The range of services offered by production companies is vast and your choice will probably be dictated by your budget. You can use them to produce well-designed slides only, or you can hand over to them the entire organisation of your sales conference, including guest speakers and participants from around the world. This book doesn't aim to show you how to run a large-scale conference. However, I am including some suggestions here for using outside assistance that may help you to avoid some of the common pitfalls:

- *Key content* Appoint one person to be the principal point of contact within your organisation to work with the production company.

- *Advance planning* Contact the professionals as early as possible. If you are planning a large conference in a major city, contact them even before you have decided the date, as they may be able to help with your choice of venue.

- *Ask questions* The professionals may talk in jargon and abbreviations but don't be put off by that. If you don't understand what they are talking about, ask.

- *Allow sufficient time* You will naturally want to include the latest sales figures or the most recent data in your presentation, but don't make this an excuse for not providing the production company with scripts in plenty of time. If necessary, you can add the final figures later, but at least you can avoid the expense of having their staff working overtime.

- *Late changes cost money* Nothing is impossible, but everything costs money. Ensure that everyone, and that includes your chairperson, has prepared a script that won't need eleventh-hour changes. Remember that slides will be prepared to illustrate certain points in the script and if the words are changed, the visual may have to be scrapped.

SUMMARY

- Decide whether you really need visuals and make sure that you're using them for the right reason.

- Make visuals simple, colourful, consistent and relevant so that they add value.

- Visuals should visually aid the audience to follow and understand your talk and not distract from it.

7

Looking Professional When Using Visual Aids

'We are what we repeatedly do.
Excellence then is not an art but a habit.'
ARISTOTLE

In this chapter I offer you some fail-safe suggestions on using visual aid equipment and also some hints on which type of visual aid to use for specific events. The two visual aids used mostly commonly these days are laptop computers with data projectors and flip charts. You might still occasionally need to use an overhead projector if there are no funds to invest in newer technology, so I have covered this, together with 35mm slides.

Flip Charts

Flip charts are most suitable for informal groups of twenty or fewer people, and are used most effectively during the course of a presentation to do the following:

- record information given by members of the audience;
- calculate;

- show organisational change;

- illustrate a process or model;

- highlight and summarise essential points.

They can also serve as visual reminders – a listener who has been distracted can tune back in by glancing at the flip chart. In addition, the main points given on a flip chart can help you to summarise at the end of your talk. Consider using two flip charts, one to display the key ideas, the other as a scribbling pad.

I have seen a speaker at an internal meeting open her talk with a question to the audience: 'Now what do you think are the chief factors we need to consider about our new timetable?' As the audience responded she noted their points on the flip chart and addressed each in turn. Be sure you can anticipate what your listeners might say. You must also show why you are not accepting all of their answers – for example, 'I'm not going to write down holiday schedules because we will be discussing these in more detail at the meeting planned for Friday afternoon.' If you genuinely want a contribution from the listeners, it's important that your body language indicates this. Stand relaxed, but ready to write, making encouraging eye contact with each listener.

Using a flip chart in brainstorming sessions is helpful as it enables all the points to be visible to your group. As each sheet is completed you can tear it off and stick it on the walls around the room so that you make up a complete picture.

Hints on using a flip chart

I suggest you always carry your own marker pens as they can dry out quickly and those supplied may not write well; also, you can be sure that you have the right thickness and colour for your purpose.

You can prepare the flip chart in advance, but if the paper is thin, only write on every other page, otherwise some of your audience will attempt to decipher what is written on the next page. Use block capitals at least 5cm tall in a variety of colours to ensure that your visual is easy to read and attractive to look at. Remember to hide your prepared flip chart until it is relevant so that it creates maximum impact. Flip chart pads are usually 60cm by 80cm, but they are also available in larger sizes and a smaller variety for use with desktop easels. If you are drawing graphs or working out calculations seek out paper printed with faint squares – they are invisible to the audience but make it easier to write in a straight line.

The height of some easels is adjustable. I remember seeing a short speaker struggling with a large piece of flip chart paper, trying to fold it over against a strong current from an air-conditioning duct. Practise turning the pages over and if there is any difficulty, lower the easel or arrange for one of your listeners to help you at the appropriate time.

Use a paper-clip or fold over the corner of the page to indicate your next visual or a visual to which you want to refer back during the course of your talk.

Some speakers are reluctant to make use of a flip chart in front of the audience or during the course of their talk because they fear they won't be able to write clearly or, worst of all, their spelling will let them down. Use lined paper to overcome the first difficulty, and bad spellers can always admit their weakness and ask for help from the audience. If you can anticipate some of the words you'll need write them in pencil at the side of the flip chart; your audience won't be able to see them and you'll have a crib to refer to. If you are using the flip chart to summarise your main points, prepare it in pencil to be certain of the correct spacing of your letters and words. If you make a mistake while preparing your flip chart you can either tear off the sheet and start again or use white correcting fluid over the error, wait until it dries and write over it.

Writing clearly and quickly on a flip chart in front of an audience is not easy so, if you're planning to use it frequently, find time to practise as it's a skill that can be learnt.

How to look really professional

- Always remove the previous speaker's chart.

- Stand to one side of the easel, on the left if you're right-handed and on the right if you're left-handed, so that as you write you are not obstructing the audience's view; this position allows you to glance over your shoulder occasionally, to keep eye contact with your listeners. Also stand to one side of the easel if you are indicating points on the flip chart.

- Don't hang on to the easel for support.

- Never write and speak at the same time. This is one of the most difficult rules to follow but remember that anything that you say while you are writing will not be heard by your listeners; they will be concentrating on what you're writing and not listening, and your voice will be muffled as it will be directed at the flip chart and not at your audience.

- Don't hold a marker pen in your hand when you're not writing.

- Look at the audience and not at the flip chart. Speakers break this rule more often than any other because eye contact with the audience is difficult and looking at a familiar flip chart is comforting. Learn to overcome this problem and stand square to the audience and not half-turned to the flip chart.

Laptop Computers

Laptop presentations are used by many speakers who are familiar with the basic elements of creating PowerPoint slides. However, some speakers rely on their assistants to produce slides, while others depend on their more technically minded colleagues to set up the equipment.

If you are in either of these categories, I recommend that you bring yourself up to speed with PowerPoint as it will give you the confidence to know that you will be able to cope if something goes wrong. A member of the audience may help you out in such a case, but your credibility and self-esteem will have been dented. Spend time becoming familiar with the software programme and the equipment to run it.

The advantages of using laptop visuals are:

- new material can be incorporated, for instance up-to-the-minute, accurate sales figures;

- presentations can be customised easily;

- the transitions between slides are smooth;

- text builds are hassle-free and key points can be highlighted;

- sound and video clips can be added;

- colour, backgrounds and professional templates add impact.

The disadvantages are also all the points listed above. Presenters (and their audiences) can get carried away with the technology, so instead of adding value, the visuals hijack the presentation (see also page 76).

Equipment

Laptop computer

The rule of thumb for laptops is simple – get the fastest you can lay your hands on and always run it from the mains. I shall resist the temptation to recommend specifications because the IT world moves so rapidly that my suggestions will be almost instantly out of date.

Ensure that you have a video display card if you want to show clips and a video capture card so that you can input from TV, video or your own camcorder. You will also need a sound card. Be aware of infringing copyright laws if you use audio or video that is not in the public domain. You could fire up Netscape Navigator or Internet Explorer to show off your company's website. Sales presentations are often now designed to be self-navigated or guided by the sales person on the end of the phone to the prospect. The presentation is built with many branches or options, which can be followed depending on interests and needs, along the same lines as a pull-down menu on a website.

Projector

Data or LCD projectors are portable and usually used with laptops. It is possible to download your presentation on to a memory stick or USB connector and eliminate the need for the laptop. However, some functions, such as transitions, will not be projected.

DLP (Digital Light Processing) projectors, particularly the three-chip design, give a better, clear picture, but you should aim for 750/800 ANSI lumens (which is the brightness measurement) for an audience of approximately twenty. Some companies prefer to hire in projectors when they are needed as the technology is improving rapidly and a purchased projector can quickly be superseded by later models. Be sure to have an appropriate stand for the projector. See also page 104.

Screen

If you are presenting to a couple of people you can do it directly from the laptop. Ensure that the screen is not catching any reflected light and that the image is visible to your listeners.

In the absence of a screen, or in a small space, you may wish to project directly on to a plain wall; however, you should expect a reduction in the quality of the image.

Where you position the screen will depend on how dominant you want your slides to be. If you are illustrating 80 per cent of your presentation, place the screen centrally; if only 20 per cent of your talk has visual support, *you* should be centre stage. Place the screen to your left, which makes it easier for the audience to look from you to the screen, and read visuals from left to right. See the layouts on pages 228–9.

For larger, more formal presentations you may wish to use rear screen projection. The projector is placed behind the screen and is invisible to the audience. A special opaque screen is needed for back projection, together with a projector with a reverse image feature.

Plasma screens are installed in some meeting rooms and used as alternatives to projectors, and also double up as monitors for video conferencing. They are not portable and therefore cannot replace the data projector for off-site presentations. Although the picture quality is very high, they can only be used for audiences of under fifteen people because of their size.

How to look really professional using a laptop with a data projector

- Always make a hard copy of your visuals in case of equipment failure.

- Put your presentation on *two* CD-ROMs or memory sticks in case one of them has a fault.

- You may wish to send your presentation by email over your company's Intranet if you are presenting internally, but are away from your home base.

- If possible put your presentation on the hard drive of your laptop to save time and hiccups with downloading the disk.

- Ensure that you have an extension lead if your presentation is away from your home base and a plug adapter if you are going overseas.

- Print out your visuals six to a page and number them as they appear in the slide sorter. This will enable you to locate a specific slide rapidly, perhaps in order to answer a question from the audience. On your keyboard you simply press the number of the slide followed by Enter to locate and project the slide. With a printout of your slides you can quickly decide which slides to omit if your time slot is reduced.

- Allow double the time you think is sufficient to set up.

- Ensure that the laptop is connected to your projector and switch on the projector before you start up the computer.

- If when you switch on your laptop you notice that the presentation is only projected on the screen you will need to make an adjustment. On your laptop, press Fn and F5 (on some laptops F4 – look for the icon of two screens on one of the F keys), and the visual will appear on the laptop only. Press Fn and F5 again and it will appear on the laptop and the screen. Being able to block out the slide on the big screen is particularly useful if by accident you come out of your presentation or there is a technical hitch. You will be able to sort it out on the laptop without the audience seeing your frantic efforts.

- Switch off the screensaver on your laptop.

- The projected image should fill the screen and not overlap on to the wall or ceiling behind, nor should you have a keystone effect (where the bottom part of the slide is narrower than the top) – use the controls on the projector for adjustment.

- Experiment with the colour and contrast controls on the projector to get the best picture and, if necessary, switch off any overhead light in the room that shines directly on the screen.

- Check the volume of your speakers if the presentation contains an audio element.

- Run through your presentation at least once with a data projector, as colour that works on a computer may change when projected.

- It is unnecessary to show a continuous stream of slides. Some areas of your presentation may require you to be the sole point of focus. Alternatively, you may be asked a question and wish to remove a slide while you answer. Press the B key on your keyboard and the screen will go black. Press it again and the image will reappear.

- Use a remote control if possible, so that you are not tied to the laptop when you want to advance slides. Always carry spare batteries for the remote.

- If you switch off the projector when it is not needed, for instance during a lunch break, remember to allow one minute for it to warm up before you project your next slide.

Overhead Projector

Many organisations have replaced overhead projectors with laptops, but you do come across them in situations where there is a limited budget. They are suitable for small and medium-sized audiences, and the slides are easy to make on a computer using PowerPoint. The slides are printed out on to acetate, also called transparencies.

Projector

Very often projectors are placed on trolleys that fit them snugly but leave no space on which to put the transparencies. Try to find a low table with adequate room for the projector and the transparencies, and hopefully you will be able to project sufficiently high so that the top arm of the projector doesn't interfere with the audience's view. When the transparencies are being projected you may need to step to one side to avoid blocking the screen. Get a colleague to check visibility when you are alongside the projector. See 'Important Hints for Projecting Slides', page 107.

Using transparencies

Place a transparency on the projector and aim to fill the screen, avoiding an uneven white border of light. You may have to move the projector backwards or forwards to adjust the picture size. Turn the knob on the vertical column to adjust the focus.

Screen

Try to match the screen size to the size of the audience and place it at least two screen widths from the front row and not more than five from the back row. Place it across a corner of the room rather than in the centre of a wall (see pages 228–9 for seating diagrams), and make sure that the top of the screen can be tilted forwards towards the projector to avoid the keystone effect (this is when the top of the projected slide is wider than the bottom – if it's not possible to adjust the screen, place something under the front of the projector to raise it). Bright lights and sunlight shining on the screen will mar the picture, so make arrangements to avoid them.

How to look really professional using an overhead projector

- Always switch off the projector before removing your transparency. The speaker who waves her transparency over the projector is providing a minor distraction and a blank screen is unpleasant to look at. If you have a series of slides simply move the next slide into place without switching off.

- Point at the transparency and not at the screen. I have seen a speaker standing on tiptoe and apologising for not being able to reach the furthest corner of the screen to indicate some vital statistic, when all he had to do was to point at the transparency on the projector.

35mm Slides

It is important to remember that 35mm slides are not flexible: once the carousel is loaded, it is not possible to change the order or omit slides. However, you can project 35mm slides more quickly and more smoothly than using an overhead projector.

Slides have the disadvantage of needing a darkened room, making it difficult for the audience to take notes or for the speaker to see the audience; you should arrange for a spotlight to shine on you during the slide show so that your listeners can see you and also to help you read your notes. Because of the need to change the lighting, your slides should not be sprinkled throughout your talk but shown together in one section.

If you are arranging a meeting or conference using 35mm slides, here is some of the equipment you will need.

Screen

Place the screen in the centre of the room and use a remote control to change slides. If this is not available you will need to work in close harmony with the projectionist to indicate the moment to move from one slide to another. For informal groups, you may choose to project the slides on to a suitable blank wall.

Projector

Place the projector directly in front of the screen, making sure that it doesn't obstruct the audience's view. The focus adjustment is generally located on the front of the projector around the lens, and you should ensure that there is a spare bulb and enough extension cable to reach the socket. Consider using two projectors to avoid the unprofessional blank screen at the point where the slide changes over. A twin dissolved unit adds an efficient touch to the presentation, and can be hired at a relatively low cost. See 'Important Hints for Projecting Slides', page 107.

Slides

A carousel holds eighty slides, so try to avoid having eighty-five and have your slides mounted professionally in hinged cases with glass that can be easily cleaned. These ensure that the slide stays in focus, whereas the cheaper type tends to move in the projector.

Carousel

When you load your slides, stand by the carousel, looking towards the front of the room, following the beam of the projector's light, and hold the slide above the tray in a position so that you can read it. Place the slide in the carousel upside down, so that the top of the slide enters first. Many speakers make the mistake of turning the slide over before loading, which causes it to be projected back to front.

How to look really professional using 35mm slides

- Number all your slides and make sure your script is marked so that you know where each should appear.

- Double-check that the carousel is correctly loaded.

- Practise your entire presentation at least twice, with the projectionist or by using remote control.

- Mark on the floor the exact position of the projector in case it is moved after the rehearsal.

- Use a pointer to indicate particular areas of interest, but put it down when not in use and resist the temptation to use it as a walking stick, or to conduct the audience like an orchestra.

Important Hints for Projecting Slides

Try to avoid switching on the projector without a visual in place. A blank, bright screen attracts everyone's eyes. If you doubt this, stand in front of a group and switch on the projector without a slide. You will see all eyes focused on the screen and, until you project a visual, everyone's mind will be in a state of anticipation for what is to come.

You will need to allow enough time for your audience to absorb the content of your slide. I am often amazed that speakers who have obviously spent considerable time on producing excellent visuals leave them on view for such a short time.

Remember, they may be very familiar to you, but the audience is seeing them for the first time and they require an adequate period to understand their full significance.

Before you show a complex visual, explain to the listeners what it is intended to illustrate.

Once the slide is shown to the audience allow a few moments of silence before commenting on it. The sense of sight is more powerful than the sense of hearing (one of the advantages of using visual aids), so your listeners will be looking and not listening.

You may need to explain the visual. This is not always necessary but it may speed up the audience's comprehension; certainly the main point of the visual should be repeated to help to reinforce it.

Try to avoid looking at the screen yourself. Many professional speakers, who should know better, find the screen has a magnetism that forces them to keep looking at it. I have even seen speakers continue to look at the screen after they have switched off the projector. Your attention should be on the audience, even when they are looking at the screen. So, what happens if you suddenly get a blank mind and can't remember what is shining out behind you? Look at your laptop or overhead projector. It's as well to remember that no one will be persuaded by the back of your head – they prefer to see your face all the time.

It's advisable not to walk between the projector and the screen. You will lose authority as your slide will be projected on to your face and the light will dazzle you.

If you need to indicate on an overhead projector use a pen (with a flat side that you can place on the projector), not your shaking hand. Use a pointer to indicate with a data or 35mm projector.

Try to remove the visual as soon as it is no longer relevant. If necessary use a logo slide when there is a section of your presentation that does not require visuals.

Using transitions on a laptop will ensure that your information only appears when it is relevant. Fade down bullet points as you move on.

Last but not least never assume equipment will not be touched, moved or adjusted if you leave the room.

SUMMARY

- Take time to familiarise yourself with the equipment.

- Rehearse in situ, including setting up and closing down.

- Always have a back-up plan in case of equipment failure.

PART TWO

Presentation

8

Avoiding a Blank Mind

'Speeches are like babies – easy to conceive and
difficult to deliver.'
PAT O'MALLEY

Your talk has developed from ideas in your head to words on
the page, but until you have conveyed these thoughts to the
audience you will not have achieved your objective. In this
chapter I describe four methods of delivery that you can use
and explain the advantages and disadvantages of each of them.

Reading a Paper

Reading from a paper is my least favourite method of delivery
and I think you should try and avoid it. It is particularly ineffective for small groups, but there are many disadvantages
whatever the size of the audience.

To be an impressive speaker you need to have sincerity,
enthusiasm and vitality, and unless you are a professional actor
you will find it difficult to express these emotions when you are
reading.

Here are some of the other disadvantages:

- You can't keep good eye contact – one of the essential elements of effective speaking.

- Your body language is restricted – your script is like a ball and chain limiting your movements.

- You will sound unnatural and therefore insincere.

- Depending on a script will mean you are limiting your potential to be a convincing and confident speaker.

There may be some occasions when you can't avoid reading a script, so in Chapter 16 I have included advice on writing spoken English and techniques to improve your reading aloud skills.

Memorising Your Script

I believe that memorising your script is another method to be avoided because all your energy will be directed inwards instead of outwards to your audience. They will feel an invisible barrier and a lack of warmth, even if they don't understand the reason for it. Your talk will sound mechanical and will lack the vital ingredients of *enthusiasm* and *spontaneity*.

I remember seeing a speaker who had a very eloquent and impressive style, with well-balanced sentences and a wide vocabulary, suddenly start to stumble halfway through his speech. He referred to his notes but never regained his confidence. It transpired that he had a photographic memory and had attempted to memorise the entire speech, but when his memory had let him down, he couldn't find his place in the script. In a second he lost credibility as he changed from being a fluent and articulate speaker to being hesitant and uncertain.

Although you may think you know your talk word for word, nerves can have an adverse effect on your memory and, unless you are very quick-thinking, you could find yourself floundering. By all means memorise certain passages that you are anxious to include, but don't rely on your memory for the entire speech. If you are only saying a few sentences you may well find that you can remember them – however, you might decide to have a small cue card at hand with the main points just in case you lose your way.

So, if you shouldn't read a speech and you shouldn't memorise it and you can't make up an entire talk off the top of your head, how can you put across your message?

Speaking Extemporaneously (or Planned Improvisation)

This is the most effective delivery style as it has all the benefits of impromptu speaking and none of the drawbacks of reading. Your talk is prepared carefully, with a punchy beginning, a logical structure and a conclusive ending; it's well rehearsed and you can use brief outline notes to give you the confidence to sound enthusiastic, behave with vitality and look at the audience with sincerity.

What happens if I get a blank mind?

All speakers who speak extemporaneously have a safety net and you must decide which type is most appropriate for you and your talk.

There are several possibilities. However, if you have dipped into this chapter without having read Part One, you may want to look at it now, as you will find it easier to understand what follows.

Using your mind map as a safety net

You will recall that on the mind map (see page 25) you put all possible facts and details about the subject of your talk and you didn't attempt to evaluate them or fit them into a structure. At the next stage you studied the map to choose the ideas most appropriate for helping you achieve your objective in regard to your particular audience.

If you are using the mind map as your safety net you'll find the original map contained many fruitful ideas that were later discarded, so you will need to draw a second map that shows only the essential arguments and material. Draw the ideas in a logical sequence following a clockwise direction so that when you are delivering your talk you can simply glance occasionally at the map to reassure yourself that you are including all the salient points.

A mind map has the advantage of being visual and displays your talk in its entirety. This is helpful if you need to cut or condense during the course of your presentation. The details of your talk should be well known to you, so you will only need a prompt of a few words if your memory fails you. Sometimes your mind may go blank between ideas; you finish one point and suddenly realise you can't remember what comes next. You only need a nudge or a few words to set you off again. Often it's the structure or the sequence of points you forget, not the ideas themselves. The mind map can put you back on track when this happens.

You may feel that a mind map could be ambiguous or confusing – supposing you lost your place and couldn't remember which path you were on? If you are unsure of the benefit of the mind map as a safety net consider some of these other prompts you can use when speaking without a script.

Your script as a safety net

In your preparation, you will have moved through the following stages:

- researching the audience;
- setting an objective;
- drawing a mind map;
- choosing a path.

I suggested in Chapter 3 that you may not need to write out a full script, but simply to note key ideas on cards; if you don't work with a script, you can't use it as a prompt. However, if you do have a written script this doesn't mean reading every word.

Use a coloured pen to underline the key ideas so that they are conspicuous. As you rehearse, you should aim to describe each idea and link it with the next one without reading or memorising all the words in between. Simply glance at it from time to time to check the next point. If you employ alternative phrases and words during your practice, your talk will be fresh and different every time you rehearse. Using a script in this way increases your ability to speak fluently and decreases your dependence on the prepared text.

The key ideas are highlighted to assist you to follow your predetermined structure but you have the freedom to use your own choice of words to travel from one point to the next. Practise speaking around each point and don't be tempted to rely on the script; you should only use it as a guide to your destination and not as a vehicle to take you there.

Using confidence cards as a safety net

The mind map can sometimes be misleading and a full script as a safety net can be too detailed; confidence cards combine the advantages of both without the drawbacks of either.

You can prepare confidence cards directly from your mind map, or from your full script. Remember that confidence cards should never contain full sentences as you don't read the cards – you only glance at them in moments of uncertainty. Eloquent phrases and clever ideas will only confuse you. Sometimes clients tell me that because of their nerves they can't see what is written on their cards, but frequently I find that their cards are closely covered with fully written sentences. These are not a help – they are a hindrance.

How to write confidence cards

Look at your script or mind map and mark the key points in red; next check the links you have used to move from one point to another and mark these in blue. If you have included anecdotes and illustrations, mark these in green. This will provide the skeleton of your talk.

Using 102mm by 152mm index cards write out in capital letters your key points, your links and your illustrations in the order in which they appear in your talk. Write on one side of the cards only.

If you are working from a full script, you must be very self-disciplined to avoid including all your persuasive phrases and scintillating sentences. Only single key words will help you.

Remember it's *your* speech with *your* ideas so you don't have to absorb and learn a host of alien concepts that you might forget. You only need to learn the sequence of ideas and the links between them to give a good talk.

I restrain myself from writing too much on my cards by considering whether I would be able to continue my talk without a particular word or phrase. Often I find that I reject it because it's not central to my talk. I have included it because it was a particularly clever turn of phrase.

The test for the effectiveness of your confidence cards is how few words you have on them, not how many.

Why cards?

I suggest you use 102mm by 152mm cards, because they are less distracting than paper. You can hold them in your hand, or rest them on the lectern or table, and you will look professional. Should you suffer from trembling hands, cards won't reveal this as much as a flapping piece of paper would. Remember to number the cards so that should you drop them this will not prove a calamity.

What's on them?

As well as reducing your talk to key words and ideas, on your confidence cards you can add instructions to yourself such as 'smile', 'look at the audience', 'stand still', etc., and you can mark the point where you want to use a visual aid or write on a flip chart.

Only two full sentences

Although it's essential to mark only key words on your cards, there are two exceptions to this rule. To give a strong framework you can write out in full the opening and closing sentences of your talk. You will probably find that your anxiety is at its highest point immediately before you speak and it's reassuring to see in front of you the exact words with which you'll begin. Similarly, you will need a clear end to your talk and if the final sentence is written out in full, you will be able to resist the temptation to run past the finishing post.

Memorising the opening and closing sentences can also be a boost to your confidence and will enable you to make positive eye contact with your listeners at the two periods in your talk when you know you are likely to have their maximum attention.

You should also write out in full any quotations you intend to include as it's essential to use the exact words.

> Remember   3
>
> ## II COST/ TIME RECRUITMENT
> ## - ADVERTISEMENTS
> ## - SEC. & MANAGER'S TIME
> ## - NON-PRODUCTIVE TIME
>
> FLIP CHART
>
> RECRUIT 1 SEC. = £560
> 30 x 560 = £16,800
> eg Post-room clerk 5 in 12 mths

Speaker's prompt card

What are the advantages?

Using confidence cards will help you to:

- Sound natural – because you will be choosing your own words as you speak;

- Be confident – because you will have a safety net in the event of a blank mind;

- Look at the audience – because you won't need to read a script;

- Use expressive body language – because you will be free to move.

Show *sincerity, enthusiasm* and *vitality*.

If you have to give the same talk several times confidence cards will allow you to use a different vocabulary and even different illustrations for each audience. This will help you to remain fresh and spontaneous and prevent the material from becoming repetitious for you.

Suppose I leave something out?

People on my training courses who have not had experience of using confidence cards tell me they are concerned that they may leave something out. Sometimes a participant on a course will resume his place, having given his presentation, and as the other participants are congratulating him he shakes his head, saying, 'No, no, it wasn't any good, I forgot to say ...'

My response is, 'So what?' If you omit a passage, no one is aware of it but you. It will probably be a tiny percentage of the whole and although you would have liked to include it, rarely will such an omission affect the total impact of your talk. Don't dwell on what you have forgotten – instead, accept the praise for what you have remembered.

One word of warning – if you discover that you have omitted a passage while you are still speaking, beware of trying to backtrack in order to include it. You may confuse the audience. Should you feel that it is essential and cannot be omitted, don't apologise for leaving it out. Simply refer to it as an additional point that your listeners may want to consider, and remember to put it into context so that the audience can follow your structure. Often listeners know that their concentration is poor and even if you announce that you have four points to make and fail to include one of them, the audience will believe that the error is theirs and that they have misheard you.

If you have never used notes before and have always depended upon a full script, I urge you, during your practice sessions, to dispense with your script and try a few dry runs using only your cards. You will feel a great sense of freedom after your second or third attempt. If you are not prepared to risk dispensing with your script, try reducing some of it to key words and bullet points. This will enable you to look at the audience and talk spontaneously from time to time.

Pitfalls to avoid with confidence cards

Using confidence cards effectively will allow you to be an enthusiastic and sincere speaker but beware of these pitfalls:

- Don't shuffle or play with them during your talk.

- Don't keep staring at them to avoid looking at the audience.

- Don't use fillers – 'eh, umm, you know, I mean' etc. – as you choose your words; remember the power of the silent pause.

Visual aids as a safety net

Provided you plan to stand or sit close to the projector, you can write prompts to yourself on the notes pages of your PowerPoint presentation. A few key words should be sufficient to provide a structure that you can follow easily. If this is your preferred method of prompt, read the advice about confidence cards (see page 118), as many of the recommendations given there also apply to visual aids.

Visual aids can act as a prompt but beware of using unimaginative and wordy slides simply to provide cues for yourself during your talk. In Chapter 6 I recommended that they should contain a minimum of words to be effective. Using words on the visual aid merely as a prompt is a misuse of it and instead of providing clarity for the audience will only confuse them as they will be attempting to read your slide instead of listening to you. A good guideline to remember is that during a talk, words are for speaking not for reading.

I sometimes use a visual during a training session on body language. I draw a stick man on the flip chart, and as I emphasise the importance of eye contact and using hand gestures, I indicate these parts on the drawing. This helps to reinforce my message and also acts as a visual prompt for me.

Using a combination of creative visuals and confidence cards provides you with an effective safety net which won't prevent you from looking at your audience and using appropriate gestures.

SUMMARY

- Avoid reading copious notes and try to speak extemporaneously.

- Prepare for a blank mind and choose a suitable safety net.

- Practise several times aloud, preferably with a tape recorder or on video.

9

Killing Your Nerves with Kindness

'There are only two types of speaker: those who get
nervous and liars.'
MARK TWAIN

'Before they get up, they do not know what they are going
to say; when they are speaking, they do not know what
they are saying; and when they have sat down, they do
not know what they have said.'
CHURCHILL (on Lord Charles Beresford, 1912)

Once you have decided the best way to deliver your talk the
next thing to consider is how to handle those inevitable
nerves. You may find it difficult to believe, but even the most
accomplished performers suffer from nerves. Recently the
actor Hugh Grant admitted that he suffered from what he
called 'camera fright.' Prime Minister Tony Blair said that he
still gets nervous when public speaking, 'I think it's a pre-
requisite of doing the job properly.' Actor Daniel Day Lewis
once left the stage during a performance at the National
Theatre because of nerves. Actor, comedian and writer
Stephen Fry actually left the country because of the pressures
of performing in front of audiences.

When a speaker fails to feel nervous, the chances are that the speaker has become complacent and boring. You need nerves to give you sparkle, but what you don't want are nerves that cripple you and prevent you from performing well. So, in this chapter, I don't show you how to kill the butterflies but I do show how you can train them to fly in formation.

First Catch Your Butterflies

I want to look at what makes you nervous, how it feels and how you can overcome it.

Immediately I see that I have set myself an impossible task. How can I know what makes *you* nervous and how it feels for *you*? So, you're going to have to help me. You will need some paper and a pen to get the most out of this chapter. Pause for a moment in your reading and make a list of all the physical and mental manifestations of nerves you have when you speak to a group of people. This is your list. If you have trouble remembering, think of the last time you were embarrassed – *where* did it affect you? In your face? Your stomach? Your hands?

You might find that just thinking about feeling nervous produces some of the symptoms. If so, observe them and try to measure your level of anxiety on a scale of one to ten. One is the lowest level of anxiety and ten is the highest level. Speaking in public is never a ten because if you were trapped in a locked car on a level crossing with a train bearing down on you, facing instant death, you would probably be feeling worse. Speaking in public might feel like death but you wouldn't die; it won't kill you. In a survey in the US, 3,000 people were asked to list their ten worst fears and speaking in public came out as number one ahead of death, financial ruin, spiders and snakes. You may sympathise with this view but do remember that death is permanent and making a fool of yourself in public is not.

What Colour is Fear?

Do you think of a colour when you think of fear? No? Try and describe in words what your nervousness actually looks like: what colour is it, what shape does it have, does it move? Take it out of your body and look at it. Keep it there for a moment while I list some of the symptoms that my clients have come up with over the years:

- shaking knees, palpitating heart and churning stomach;
- tight throat and unable to swallow, dry mouth or too much saliva;
- wet palms, feeling very hot, blushing and feeling cold;
- blank mind, unable to focus on audience or notes and feeling faint;
- stuttering, shortness of breath, nervous laugh and trembling voice.

You may recognise many of these and you might even suffer from some symptoms that aren't on the list. I find that I sweat a lot when I am nervous, but fortunately only under my arms and not on my face so that it doesn't show. I also find that my heart beats extra fast and that my stomach churns.

The colour of my fear and nervousness is black and dark green and looms about me in a threatening cloud and I think it's laughing at me, but you know a strange thing happens when I actually have the courage to look at it. It seems to become smaller. Try to examine your nervousness without allowing it to threaten you. Just acknowledge its presence without any dread. Just think about the feeling and try to put it outside yourself. I know it's not easy, but the more you try, the less frightening it will become.

What Makes You Nervous?

I can't answer that question for you, so again you will have to make a list for yourself of all the disasters that could happen to you. *List as many fears as you can.* Remember it's the fears that are making you nervous. Imagine you are in your next speaking situation and are feeling terrified, or imagine that you have been asked to speak, or even that you are in a meeting and want to speak but something is holding you back. What is it?

Is it fear of any of these things happening?

• Forgetting what you want to say. Not making sense. Being boring.

• People disagreeing, asking difficult questions, even getting up and walking out.

• Your boss thinking that you are an idiot.

• Letting down your subordinates, colleagues and friends.

• Being judged and found wanting – by yourself or others.

You may see from your own list that some of your fears are not unique. It's quite reassuring on my courses to find that many fears are shared; even the person who appears to be most confident worries about looking foolish. Everyone has an insecure centre. The next time you see a good speaker, ask her how she felt before her speech and, if she is prepared to be honest, I am sure you will find that she, too, suffers from nerves.

The great truth

Now we have discovered the great truth of public speaking –
everyone suffers from nerves and everyone is frightened of
looking foolish. Think about that for a minute because it's very
reassuring. You are not any different from anyone else. You
may be thinking that if other people felt as nervous as you, they
could not speak as well as they do. You may be thinking that
your nerves are worse than anyone else's. They are not. The
nerves are the same, but the difference may be that you have
not learnt to control your nerves – they are controlling you.

Negative thoughts or positive power?

Do you dislike feeling nervous? You may think it's absurd to
ask such a question, but try to welcome your anxiety because
you need it to be a good speaker. It is the force that drives your
motor and without it you will be dull and uninspiring; you
need to harness its power to give you positive energy or it will
dominate you and cause crippling panic. Regard it as part of
the equation in the same way that you regard other feelings.
Before taking off your jacket you feel hot; before eating you
feel hungry; before going to bed you feel tired; and before
speaking in public you feel nervous.

What are you really afraid of?

Earlier I asked you to look at the shape and colour of your
nerves. This may have been difficult, but now I'm going to
show you how to get to know and understand your nervousness, so that you can take the first steps towards gaining control
and turning negative nerves into positive power. But I can only
do this if you are willing to cooperate in a painful exercise. If
you are reading this in a bookshop, I suggest you go to the cash

desk immediately, because you will need a quiet half-hour by yourself if the next section is to have any lasting effect on you. Take the book home and only open it again when you know you can concentrate on it.

How to Control Your Nerves

Imagine that you are at your next speaking occasion. You are about to begin speaking, you look around and you see people waiting for you to start. How does it feel? What is your level of anxiety? As you stand or sit there, what are your fears? *What is your worst fear*? Can you identify it? What is the most awful thing that could happen to you? Think about it in detail because it's about to happen. Don't close your mind to it, just let it happen and feel the total horror and your inability to control the situation. It is getting worse and you can do nothing. Dwell for a few moments on the feelings that you are experiencing as you imagine your greatest fear.

After a time you do manage to get out of the more public arena and you find that you are shaking all over. Never, never again you say to yourself, never again will they get me to speak in front of an audience. You feel humiliated, mortified and ashamed. Examine the horror and dwell on it – remember this is only in your imagination so you can escape from it at any stage, but it might be best if you stayed with it for a few moments more. Imagine how you would feel, what you would say, what you would do, how you would live through that terrifying experience. Put down this book so you can concentrate on your worst fear. If you can force yourself to face up to your worst possible fear, you will be going a long way towards controlling your nerves.

On one of my courses I had a manager who feared the audience walking out – he gave presentations to audiences of 150 people – and imagined that as he was speaking first one person and then another and then small groups began standing up and making for the exit. He was left with five or six people scattered about a large hall. He imagined the whole scene, how he eventually left the stage and how he felt afterwards.

A young woman confided to me that she was always unable to ask questions when she attended her evening class because she was convinced the lecturer would be able to tell she was stupid and hadn't listened properly. She imagined the training room and the tutor who challenged her. She imagined her bumbling answer. She imagined the terrifying scene as the rest of the group turned and looked at her with contempt and how she felt for the rest of class and on the journey back home.

Let's go back to your most terrifying moment and imagine that already twenty-four hours have passed; but you have not discussed your disaster with anyone because it's still too painful. You feel that you can confide in a close friend maybe and you relive the whole situation. It still feels terrible, but remember you lived through it – *you did not die.*

Now look forward a month and imagine you are telling a group of friends about the experience and you find that one or two of them have had similar experiences and are very sympathetic. You are beginning to see this experience as an event in the past. Try looking forward a year, and in a pub or at a party you meet someone who was at the scene of your humiliation; he comes over and speaks to you and reminds you that he was present: 'Glad I wasn't in your shoes, if only you could have seen the look on your face – it was a scream.' You find that now a year has passed you can smile and chuckle at the memory.

You may have read quickly to the end of this section to see what the outcome was going to be. I would urge you to try this exercise and examine your worst fears and feelings. Some people have told me that they won't get a highly prized job if they don't perform well at a selection interview or that they will lose face in front of all their friends and relatives at a social occasion, others have told me that their reputation as an expert in their field might be jeopardised, or that a major contract worth millions of pounds could be lost if they fail to be persuasive. Whatever your own personal fear is, remember that it can't kill you. You will live beyond it and you may even be able to smile at the situation in the future. Bear in mind that for this exercise to work, you must not stop at the moment of the disaster, but continue through to the following twenty-four hours, the following month and the following year.

How Could You Have Coped Better?

Now that you have faced your worst fear and lived through it, try looking back at how you could have prevented it or coped better if it were to happen again. You will be tempted to ignore it, but if you can have the self-discipline to confront it, you will find that you can learn from the situation. You will gain confidence by aiming at a positive outcome.

Try reliving your worst fear again. It may be too difficult to do immediately, so read another chapter and come back to it later. On your second attempt, you can imagine yourself coping successfully with a difficult situation. Once again, imagine it in full detail; how you felt, what you said and how other people reacted. Only allow yourself to imagine a positive outcome. You may need to pause in order to choose your behaviour or find the right words; do so. This is your fantasy, so you are in charge. Of course you may also realise that your fears are ridiculous and completely groundless – that can be very reassuring.

For instance, my young female student, when challenged by the tutor in her scenario, imagined how she would smile and say, 'I have been listening and I would be grateful for some clarification on a point which I have not fully understood, either now or after the class if you prefer.' This exercise helped her to cope with her worst fear and she actually asked a question the following week which the lecturer answered with no suggestion of a putdown.

I hope that exercise has helped you to see that there is life after failure. You have faced your worst fear, coped with it and lived through it, so you can concentrate on being a success. Now you are ready to turn nerves into a positive force.

Converting Panic into Positive Power

Here are some techniques you can use to harness your nervous energy.

- Practice is your best defence against failure. Follow the suggestions in Chapter 15, and practise aloud several times in front of a long mirror so that you can become familiar with every point of your talk. Continue to the end in every practice session, because you don't want to have an over-rehearsed first half and a poor, stuttering second half. Find out as much as you can about the place where you will be speaking, seating arrangements, and any lighting and equipment, so that you feel comfortable with it.

- Try to visualise your success – create a picture for yourself of the scene immediately after you've spoken. Imagine your customers looking pleased and stimulated by what you are saying, or your board of governors nodding in agreement, or your sales force feeling motivated to work harder, or a large audience clapping enthusiastically. Whoever your listeners are, think of them reacting in a very positive manner. Try to paint a vivid picture of the situation, including your own feelings of relief and pleasure. Don't allow any negative thoughts to intrude – this is your success. The more you concentrate on this, the greater your chance of it becoming true.

- You could imagine you are an actor playing the part of a successful and confident speaker.

- Remember a good feeling – think back to a particular personal success, for example the day you passed an exam, were given a rise, got engaged to be married. Recall a day of personal achievement when you were proud of yourself and it felt good to be alive. This is your own kitty of confidence and you can tap into it whenever you feel a moment of doubt. You have achieved in the past and you can achieve in the future.

• Examine the positive aspects of nerves – ask yourself, 'What is the benefit of feeling nervous?' You may be surprised to recognise that there is actually an advantage in having butterflies.

Coping with the Physical Symptoms

So far I have considered how you can use your mind to handle your nerves; now I am looking at your body and how it reacts under stress. If you know you sweat, wear a lightweight outfit and carry a handkerchief to dab your face and hands if necessary.

If you suffer from a dry mouth limit the amount of water you drink. Instead place your tongue across your teeth and gently bite it – your saliva will begin to run. Another trick is to put the tip of your tongue at the top of your mouth and say a silent LLL sound, which will also help you to overcome a dry mouth.

Trembling hands will only be noticeable if you hold sheets of paper, so use cards and avoid trying to drink a cup of tea or coffee.

If your throat tightens up and your voice becomes restricted before you face the audience, try yawning to relax it. Lift your lips away from your teeth like an animal snarling, and open your mouth as wide as possible so that the muscles on your neck stick out and you hear a roaring in your ears. Now the yawn should start to take over and it will relax your whole face, neck and throat. You can't feel tense while yawning as it is a great relaxer, like laughing. This is definitely an exercise to practise in private and not in front of your listeners.

If you suffer from breathlessness, take deep breaths. Shallow breaths will make you sound odd and feel panicky. We take in breaths automatically, but we have to think about letting the air out, so remember to breathe in to the count of two and exhale slowly to the count of four.

I hope that some of these suggestions will work for you, but bear in mind that you are not aiming to kill the butterflies – only to control them. You need their power to be an effective speaker; so use them, don't be frightened of them and regard them as old friends.

SUMMARY

- Remember that even the most confident speaker suffers from nerves.

- The trick is not to let your nerves control you.

- Face up to your fears and prepare for a contingency.

- Learn to convert negative nerves into positive power.

- Practice kills panic.

- You *will* be successful.

10

Exercises to Help You Relax

'The brain is a wonderful organ. It works perfectly until the
moment you stand up to speak in public.'
ANON

In this chapter I describe some techniques for relaxing, which
you can practise at any time you are feeling tense, as well as in
the final moment before you begin to speak. You might even
find them useful to use before starting a difficult phone conversation.

Why is Relaxing Important?

If you can relax the tension in your muscles, you'll find that
your voice will sound less tense and more sincere, your gestures
will look natural and you will use fewer non-words and fillers.
As you learn to control your nerves and feel more confident,
your muscles will relax automatically. Here are some exercises
to help you in the process.

Getting into the Habit

I once attended a seminar on hypnotism and was selected by the hypnotist as a guinea pig. He taught me how to self-hypnotise so that when I found myself in a minor panic about being late for an appointment, I could park the car and sit for sixty seconds, and allow myself to go into a mild trance. Then I would arrive at the appointment in a more relaxed frame of mind. Unfortunately, I failed to keep practising this technique and I'm not able to use it any more, but I have retained the memory of how my body feels when it's untensed. Some people don't have that awareness. 'What do you mean relaxed – I am relaxed!' they say through clenched teeth.

EXERCISE 1 **Feel the tension**

In order to learn how to relax, you must first feel the tension. Start with your toes and curl them up as tight as possible, hold this position for 30 seconds and then release. Next, tense your calf muscles, hold for 30 seconds and release; tense your thigh muscles and buttocks, hold for 30 seconds and release; then tense your stomach and chest, hold for 30 seconds and release; tense your shoulders and neck, hold for 30 seconds and release; and finally, tense your face, hold and release. There is no need to rush this exercise – do it slowly to get the maximum benefit.

You can practise this exercise before you fall asleep at night and you'll notice a warm, tingly feeling all over your body. By being aware of the contrast between your tensed and relaxed muscles, you'll get into the habit of being able to relax at will. You'll simply recognise your tension and tell your body to let go. It's impossible to be relaxed and anxious at the same time. This exercise will only work for you in moments of high stress (like speaking to your bank manager about your overdraft) if you have practised it sufficiently in unstressed moments.

Learning to be Centred

This is fundamental to performing. An uncentred performer on the stage looks like an amateur and an uncentred speaker inevitably feels tense. Your centre, your 'point of power', is situated roughly at the solar plexus, above the navel.

EXERCISE 1 **Becoming centred**

To help you to be centred stand straight, bend your knees slightly, close your eyes and concentrate on your feet. Feel each toe digging into the floor as though you were curling your toes in sand. Now squat, keeping your feet flat on the floor. Imagine that your legs are pillars of iron connected to the centre of the earth. Rest your hands on your knees for balance. Stay there until you can feel your centre of gravity lowering to your pelvis. Rise slowly, straighten up and breathe.

EXERCISE 2 **Centring and posture**

This exercise also helps with your posture: stand sideways before a full-length mirror and bend your knees slightly. Notice how your pelvis and buttocks are out of alignment with your back. Now place your hands on your hips and gently roll your pelvis forwards, pulling your stomach in and down. Your buttocks should now be aligned directly under your back in a straight line. Now imagine a string running all the way up your spine and out of the top of your head. Let the string hold you like a puppet. This exercise centres you and enables you to use natural and graceful movements.

Five Minutes to go and in Private

EXERCISE 1 **Be a rag doll**

Allow your body to flop down from the waist and swing your arms like a rag doll. If no one can hear you say, 'I don't care – I don't care – I don't care,' as you hang loosely. This will get rid of the tension in your upper body.

EXERCISE 2 **Shoulders on parade**

Pull your shoulders right up to your ears and let go; repeat this exercise five times to release the tension in your neck and shoulders. Roll your shoulders backwards four times and forwards four times. Roll your head over your right shoulder, let it hang backwards, then bring it round over your left shoulder and finally rest your chin on your chest. Reverse the direction and repeat four times. This exercise helps to relax throat and neck muscles.

EXERCISE 3 **Wibbly wobbly**

Shake your hand from your wrist and then your arm from your shoulder and finally let all your upper body shake, including your head and lips.

EXERCISE 4 **Horse laugh**

Loosen your lips and blow through them like a horse.

EXERCISE 5 **Facial exercises**

Stretch your lips into a silent E and purse them into a silent O and now rapidly say a silent E, O, E, O. Repeat ten times. This is an excellent exercise to release those muscles around the mouth that can make you look severe when you are feeling nervous.

EXERCISE 6 **Yawn**

On page 133 I described how to make yourself yawn at will by opening your mouth as wide as you can. This will relax your neck, throat and mouth area.

One Minute to go and in Public

Tense all your muscles (not your face this time) and release. Repeat twice. Breathe deeply and exhale fully. Concentrate on your rhythmic, slow, deep breathing. Be curious about your surroundings and your audience. See how many red ties you can count. If you are in a small group, look at everyone's clothes and note the different patterns in the fabrics.

Think of a peaceful scene – walking through a pine forest, lying on a warm beach, the view from a hill across several green fields on an autumn afternoon – and feel a deep inner stillness and quiet confidence.

Think positive thoughts and you will create inner confidence for yourself.

Exercises to Aid Relaxation

EXERCISE 1 **Breathing**

Under stress breathing becomes short and shallow. By controlling your breathing pattern you can have a direct effect on your anxiety. Sit back and close your eyes. Relax your shoulders and concentrate on your breathing. Place one hand on your stomach. As you breathe in feel your stomach moving out. Slowly breathe out and feel your stomach moving in like a deflating balloon. With each breath hold it a second longer before you *slowly* breathe out. Repeat ten times for maximum benefit.

EXERCISE 2 **Facial exercises**

Push all your features to the tip of your nose five times. Push your features to the back of your head five times.

EXERCISE 3 **Shake off your nerves**

Shake your hands and arms as if you're trying to get rid of something sticking to your fingers – this will get your blood flowing. Repeat with each leg.

EXERCISE 4 **Relax your throat**

Slowly yawn. If this is difficult, open your mouth as wide as you can and keep it open – a yawn will appear from nowhere.

EXERCISE 5 **Relax your lips**

Blow through your lips to make a sound like an outboard engine on a boat. This will prevent your upper lip from sticking to your teeth when you begin to talk.

EXERCISE 6 **Mind games**

To calm your mind walk from one side of the room to the other counting backwards from twenty to one.

SUMMARY

- Learn some simple relaxation techniques.

- The more you practise loosening up when you feel tense, the more automatically your body will relax.

- As you grow more at ease with speaking in public you will appear more assured, thus creating a positive cycle of relaxation and confidence.

11

Looking Really Confident all the Time

'Great dancers are not great because of their technique; they are great because of their passion.'
MARTHA GRAHAM, dancer and choreographer

Once you have controlled your butterflies you will need to concentrate on looking confident. Unfortunately you are unlikely to make a successful speaker if you only have a good speech; in fact you could even be an effective speaker without a good speech. Some speakers can spend so long searching for the exact word, the imaginative example or the eloquent turn of phrase that they lose sight of those vital qualities that will ensure their success in front of an audience. In this chapter I describe what you need to do to make your audience think you are really confident.

We have seen that listeners are not impressed with words alone. They are impressed with:

- enthusiasm;

- vitality;

- sincerity.

The Day of Judgement

Even before you have opened your mouth, your listeners will have made several assumptions about you and, in the light of their own experience and prejudices, you will have scored plus or minus points. If you think this is unfair, consider your own internal conversation as you sit on a train or watch pedestrians from your traffic-jammed car – aren't you assessing and judging the people you see? We all do it to everyone we come in contact with, and audiences as a whole are no different; they are curious about the speaker who will be part of their lives for the duration of the talk. You never have a second opportunity to make a first impression, so whether you are entering a room for an interview, an informal meeting or an international conference, your audiences will assess you from the moment they can see you.

Look Happy!

Human beings have a very simple way of showing friendship, and yet judging by how little it is used, you would think it was very difficult and extremely expensive. Smiling at your audience says, 'I am happy to be here and I am glad you are here too.' I expect that you will be feeling the exact opposite, but that is the very reason why you should smile.

Why let everyone know you are feeling nervous? No one can see your pounding heart or churning stomach or dry mouth, so why reveal on your face the turmoil that's going on inside your body? If you think that smiling is inappropriate for your position or your subject, may I suggest that you reconsider your view because I am sure your listeners would like to welcome a friendly rather than an unfriendly speaker. Even an undertaker smiles in sympathy. You don't need an ear-to-ear grin – only an 'I am happy to be here and glad you are here too' expression.

How to Make an Entrance

You have fixed your 'I am happy' expression on your face. You enter the interview room, lecture hall or meeting venue and walk confidently to a chair or podium. You are making a first impression so let your body language say, 'Here is a worthwhile and interesting person.' In a small group, you will probably be shaking hands, always remembering to maintain eye contact and murmuring pleasantries about the weather, the cricket score or your/their journey, as you sit down. If you are speaking at a large conference centre, you will know what to expect because you will have rehearsed your entrance already. (See Chapter 16 on writing and reading scripts for conferences.)

Once settled, you can look around and take a few quiet, deep breaths. Don't look at your notes or even touch them. No amount of silent rehearsing will help you make a better speech at this stage. Instead concentrate on what is happening around you and listen to any other speakers. For many people these final few moments before they speak are the worst, but try not to let yourself be controlled by feelings of panic – you should be well rehearsed and looking forward to giving a good performance.

Why is Body Language Important?

However you look or move, you will be giving off signs to your audience as to your inner feelings – you cannot not communicate. Being aware of your particular mannerisms and nervous gestures enables you to correct them and present a confident, unselfconscious image.

In spite of my experience, I am always apprehensive standing in front of an audience, but people tell me that I look totally in control and relaxed. In fact I am in control, but I am *not* relaxed; that might sound uncomfortable to you as maybe you are aiming to be a casual, informal and unpretentious speaker. There is a line attributed to Mark Twain: 'It takes three weeks to write and perfect a good impromptu remark.' I believe that nobody is born a good speaker and that you have to work at your body language to *appear* relaxed and natural in the same way as Mark Twain worked on what appeared to be a throwaway line.

The perils of bad body language

If your inner panic shows itself in your fidgety feet and fiddling fingers, your audience will feel uncomfortable because they want and expect you to be in control. In addition, they will not have confidence in you, your ideas or your product or service. They will not believe in you, won't listen well and will quickly forget what you have said. If you look confident and believe in yourself, you will have credibility and your listeners will be eager to hear what you have to say.

As you stand facing your audience, I don't think for one moment that you will feel cool, calm and confident – I expect you will be suffering anything from mild apprehension to abject terror, depending on the extent of your experience. At this stage don't worry about your *feelings* – for at this point you want simply to appear cool, calm and confident. The rest of this chapter shows you how you can achieve this.

Eye Communication

When I am training people in effective speaking, I have to be very careful not to overrun my time when we reach the session on eye contact, because I am convinced that it is one of the most important factors towards creating a good speaker – and I love talking about the subject.

I could see it in his eyes

Looking at someone demonstrates that you are interested in them. Consider some of the common phrases about people in love: 'She only had eyes for him', 'They couldn't take their eyes off each other'. If you see two people standing together and talking, you can judge how intimate they are by observing the extent of their eye communication.

People can also use their eyes to give messages of disinterest. There is nothing more frustrating than trying to talk to someone at a party who is looking constantly over your shoulder and around the room.

Eye contact also denotes authority. Powerful people give more eye contact than those who are less confident.

We say that a person who avoids looking at us is 'shifty', but we also tell our children that staring is rude. Somewhere in between a shifty look and a stare is the correct eye contact, and it varies according to the degree of intimacy in our relationships. With eye contact, we can demonstrate our concern, love, dislike, boredom, disdain, even hatred – 'If looks could kill'. *We express our emotions through our eyes.*

Where is the audience?

I'm sure you have seen speakers who stare at the ceiling throughout their talk as if their script were written up there in large print. For variation they glance at the floor or out of the window to an imaginary listener sitting on the ledge outside.

Some speakers follow the ludicrous advice, sometimes given to novice public speakers, to find a friendly face in the audience and speak to it. After a few minutes of continuous scrutiny, the poor victim in the audience is asking, why me? The rest of the audience is feeling excluded from what appears to be an exclusive monologue; finding a friendly face is unfair both to the 'face' and to the rest of the listeners present. Avoid speaking only to the most powerful or influential person present for the same reason.

Speakers tend to look at their notes, at the back of the room, at their visual aids or even at a blank flip chart – anywhere but at the audience.

Why is it difficult to look at the audience?

Before I answer that, let me ask you a question. Do you want your audience to know that you are feeling nervous? No, of course not, and that is the reason why you find it difficult to look at them. You know instinctively that you express your emotions through your eyes, so if you don't look at them, they won't be able to see how nervous you are.

Having people looking at you is unnerving; you feel put on the spot, cornered and trapped, so you distance yourself from the situation by looking out of the window. You feel, quite illogically, that if you don't look at them, they will be able to see less of you.

What happens when you don't make eye contact

People who are interested in each other make eye contact when they are talking because they want to know how their listener is receiving their message. When you don't look at the audience, they feel (probably unconsciously) that you are not interested in them, or in their reaction to your talk; they feel the same way as you do if someone at a party talks while looking over your shoulder; they feel you don't care whether they listen or not; and because they do not feel involved by you their concentration lags.

If you don't pay attention to your audience, they will not pay attention to you

This was demonstrated to me recently, when a speaker deliberately only made eye contact with half of his audience during a forty-minute presentation. It was a medium-sized group of thirty people and afterwards when they were asked to assess the speaker, half of them found him interesting, challenging and entertaining, and the other half found him uninspiring, boring and ineffective. You can guess what had made such a radical difference to their reaction.

How is your eye contact?

During the course of your everyday life, pay attention to the eye contact other people make with you, and try and note how easy or difficult you find it to look at people when you are talking in a variety of different situations. Ask friends for feedback on your own eye contact. Practise maintaining contact for longer than usual without it becoming uncomfortable.

How to overcome your reluctance to look at the audience

Here are some games to help you gain confidence when you are speaking.

Look around the group and check the colour of your listeners' eyes. How many are wearing glasses? Do they have thick or thin eyebrows? Do their eyebrows meet in the middle? Imagine you are looking through a one-way mirror and they can't see you. These games work well with a relatively small group.

As your confidence grows, try to look at your audience's eyes and faces to see how they are reacting to your talk. In a larger group, you will need to follow a W or M shape through the audience with your eyes in order to look at every part of the hall or conference centre.

I have spoken from platforms where the bright lights aimed at the speakers made it impossible to see beyond the first row or so, but I know that it is not apparent to the audience that they are invisible, so I look out into blackness and move my eyes around as if I am looking at each person present.

What to avoid in eye contact

Once you have conquered your fear of looking at your listeners, you must improve the quality of your contact. Little, short, jerky glances are not good eye contact. Remember you are communicating your interest in your audience. Sweeping your eyes over people's faces will not convince them that you are seeking their reaction to your talk. Practise looking at each person for at least two to three seconds. If this is too difficult at first, practise on inanimate objects at home or in the office. Learn to gauge for yourself how long a two- to three-second eye rest is.

To check your eye contact after a talk, try to remember how each person looked – was the chairperson frowning? Who smiled at your anecdotes? If you can recall their facial expressions, you were making good eye contact.

Facial Communication

Eye contact is essential, but if you are frowning or appear depressed, people will not believe that you are enjoying speaking to them. So, remember your 'I am happy' expression and if you have some difficulty raising a smile when you are suffering from nerves, look slowly at your audience one by one (this is particularly effective in a small group) and imagine that they are all sitting on the toilet!

When I was first promoting my company I met a number of

rather pompous senior business people who made me feel unsure of myself and, on a couple of sales visits, I felt that I had not presented myself well because I had felt intimidated by them. On the next occasion, I wrote a note on the top of my pad to help myself to speak to the man and not be overawed by his position. I wrote 'think of him playing football in the nude, think of him playing with a toy duck in the bath'.

If you find yourself in a difficult situation where you fear your own feelings may hinder your performance, play a game to overcome your doubts. Think happy and avoid frowning at your listeners – it's not their fault that you feel nervous. You may have to exaggerate your smile if you are one of those people who can look rather sombre because, in repose, the corners of their mouths turn downwards.

Hands

When a speaker is fairly accomplished, it is often their hands that reveal apprehension.

What not to do with your hands

- *Fiddle* with rings, watch, cuff links, buttons, pens, elastic bands, paper-clips, spectacles, cuticles and nails, confidence cards, coins in pocket, pointers.

- *Touch* and pat face, hair, pockets, desk, table.

- *Clutch* back of chair, notes, side of lectern.

- *Scratch* any part of the body.

- *Hide them* behind back, in pockets, in lap, by folding arms, or by sitting on hands.

- *Point* at the audience.

- *Rub them together* in enthusiasm.

- *Wring them* in despair.

I am amazed at the range of activities that speakers find for their hands and I am sure that you have seen living examples of most of those that I have listed above.

What can you do with your hands?

Your hands do not have a separate identity – they are part of your arms and, in general, only need to move if you are making a gesture, and should only hold your confidence cards, a pointer or your wireless mouse.

Arm gestures

You will see speakers making small gestures as if their arms were paralysed to the wrist or to the elbow. It is all part of the self-consciousness of being in front of an audience. Somehow they feel that if they make small gestures, they will not be quite so visible to the audience.

Remember that your arm begins at your shoulder – always use your entire arm. Don't tuck in your elbows to your waist or make jerky, half-hearted, meaningless gestures. One of our trainers refers to this as Velcro elbows. I remember a tall woman on one of my courses who, through shyness, stood hunched up, making tiny movements with her hands. We advised her to stand tall, make eye contact and use her arms to express her enthusiasm. The result was startling – she became regal and was very impressive. Without even opening her mouth, she looked like a self-confident, interesting speaker.

When should you make gestures?

When you are not under stress, your gestures will coincide with what you are saying. You will use them to emphasise a point –

'I won't stand for this a moment longer'; you indicate a place – 'The management out there think that the staff . . .'; you can express an idea, a spiral staircase, or a size – 'We have an enormous majority . . .', 'The spare part I needed was expensive but very small.'

Some people naturally use more gestures than others; people from Latin countries tend to use more gestures than those from northern Europe. These are natural gestures and you should continue to use them if this is your style. Under stress many people wave their arms in meaningless repetitive movements as if they were trying to shake off a persistent insect. Watch yourself on video if possible, or in front of a full-length mirror, to check if you have any mannerisms you want to eliminate.

Useless gestures, as opposed to those with a purpose, reveal nervousness and become a distraction to the audience. Don't be afraid to use your arms, though, because standing rigid like a wooden soldier is as unnatural as waving your arms about unnecessarily.

What to do with your hands when you are not using your arms

If you are standing keep your hands empty and still by the sides of your body. This will feel odd, but it looks very natural. Don't, however, keep your arms glued to your sides, because when a gesture is required, your hands will only make little waving movements somewhere down by your thighs.

Some speakers feel more comfortable with their hands held lightly in front of them at waist level – if you use this position, remember not to clench your hands together so they can't escape. If you do, your gestures will eventually show themselves through jerky elbow and shoulder movements.

Other speakers like to stand with their hands lightly clasped in what is known as the fig-leaf position, slightly below the waist. Once again, be sure that your hands are free to make gestures to suit the content of your talk.

If you are holding confidence cards, be sure to gesture with the other hand. Remember you can change hands so that you are able to use both during your talk.

Position and Posture

Avoiding barriers

Facing an audience, whether it is of five, fifty or five hundred, is difficult and speakers like to hide behind desks, tables or lecterns. If you want to be an effective speaker, learn to stand totally exposed in front of your audience. Try to always stand in front of all the barriers.

Pitfalls of lecterns

I am 1.57m tall and some lecterns are 1.2m high, so how can I be a powerful speaker if my listeners can only see my head peeping over the edge of a lectern? Even if you are over 1.8m tall, standing to one side of the lectern, so that you can still refer to your notes, will allow your listeners to see all of your body. This will also make it easier for you to make natural gestures and to move around. If the lectern is fixed with a microphone, you have no choice but to stand behind it. Ask for a box to stand on if you are short so that your upper body can be seen, and ask for a radio microphone so that you are free to move away from the lectern.

Standing and sitting

I have referred to small meetings (about fifteen to twenty people) where it is customary to sit. If you can break this custom, do so, because standing gives you authority, and enables you to breathe properly, project your voice and make better eye contact. The disadvantages of sitting are:

- your chest is restricted and it is difficult to use your lungs effectively;

- your eye contact may be limited and you may be tempted to look down at your notes too much;

- your listeners may not be able to see you;

- it will be very tempting to play with pens and paper-clips on the table.

The advantages of standing are:

- you are more visible and have more authority;

- your voice projection will be better;

- you will have room to make gestures (don't lean on the table or clutch the back of the chair if you are standing behind it).

Stand tall

Act confidently, even if you are quivering inside. If you could see yourself on video, you would be surprised at how little your nerves show. Push back your shoulders and open up your chest as if you are about to begin the first day of your holiday. Remember, if you look as if you believe in yourself, your listeners will accept and retain what you say. They are on your side, so don't disappoint them. Speak to them as if you find them extremely attractive and you expect them to like you.

Finding your feet

Like hands, these creatures on the ends of our legs seem to be stimulated by nerves to act very strangely. I have seen otherwise normal men and women:

- hopping from one foot to another;
- taking two steps forwards and two steps back;
- standing on one leg;
- crossing their legs in the 'I want to go to the toilet' stance;
- rocking to and fro;
- swaying from side to side;
- flexing at the knees;
- rising up on their toes on every third word;
- rising up on their toes on every third word on a squeaky floorboard;
- sticking out one foot and 'boring for oil' with the heel;
- going on little, undirected walkabouts;
- tracking the pattern of the carpet with the curve of their shoe;
- walking up and down like a caged animal;
- standing on the sides of their shoes.

If you can identify any of these traits in your own performance, the following exercise might help you become a more grounded speaker. Imagine that you are standing in weighted boots, so that it is impossible to move without a conscious decision. You should be aiming for steady, relevant movements, not cat-on-a-hot-tin-roof jerks. You don't have to stay nailed to one spot, but you should be consciously deciding when to move to the flip chart, towards a questioner in the audience, or to pick up a prop or document, so that you are not at the mercy of your fidgeting feet.

Sometimes I find speakers who have learnt to control their feet, but compensate by swinging their hips or swaying or even leaning to one side. Stand upright on two feet a few centimetres apart, so that your hips are balanced over them and your shoulders and the rest of your body are balanced over your hips. Don't slump or lean on one foot with your hip sticking out. Think of a core of calm confidence that is beaming out from the centre of your chest. Remember to follow the rules of body language listed in the summary overleaf and you are now in a position to open your mouth and begin to speak.

Silent Presentation

Finally, if you are part of a team presentation, there will be time both before and after your talk when you will be a silent presenter. In other words, you will be part of the presentation but as a listener.

It's essential that you look interested and tuned in to your colleagues' talk. Now is not an appropriate moment to try either a last-minute mental rehearsal or an anguished recall of what you left out during your turn at the lectern. This is especially important during pitches for new business; remember that clients are assessing you as a team and your interaction (or lack of it) could be a significant factor in their decision.

SUMMARY

- Use your eyes to make contact with your listeners and show that you are interested in their reaction to you.

- Your face should say, 'I am happy to be here and I'm glad you're here too.'

- Your hands are best empty and still, avoiding the fiddles.

- Arm gestures are most effective when they start from the shoulder.

- Avoid hiding behind barriers such as table, chairs or lecterns.

- If possible stand tall, don't sit.

- Balance on both feet and wear imaginary lead-weighted boots.

- Let the beam of calm confidence shine out from your chest.

12

Finding Your Voice

'His voice sounds a little as if he is eating biscuits.'
MARIANNE MACDONALD (about Sir Ian McKellan, *Observer*
magazine, March 1998)

There is no point in looking confident and feeling relaxed if your voice lets you down.

This is not a book about elocution and I am not a drama teacher, so don't expect me to show you how to develop a deep, melodious voice, throbbing with emotion, if you normally speak in a thin, squeaky voice. No matter how you sound, you probably dislike your own voice if you have ever heard it on a tape recorder. This chapter describes techniques to help you create a more interesting voice and avoid the faults common among inexperienced speakers.

Another Great Truth

Few people like the sound of their own voice. This is because throughout your life you have heard your voice through the bone of your jaw, while everyone else (including the tape recorder) hears it straight from your mouth. Hearing yourself on tape for the first time can be a shock, so try to be objective about it. However, if you feel your voice is a serious handicap, seek professional advice from either a voice teacher or a speech therapist. I can't hear you speak so I can't judge, but of all my clients I only recommend a small percentage to seek further help. For loss of voice on a regular basis (repeat infections), huskiness/croakiness, see your doctor to ask for a referral to an ENT (ear, nose and throat) consultant or speech therapist.

Accent

Bernard Shaw said, 'An Englishman has only to say one word for another to either admire him or despise him.' Indeed, the most common complaint people have about their voice is their accent: 'I sound so posh and stand-offish,' 'I sound so common,' 'I don't like the way I pronounce my Rs,' 'My accent makes me sound unintelligent.'

Regard your accent as part of your personality and only consider changing it if you cannot be understood. There are many examples of successful men and women who have made a feature of their accent: think of Ken Livingstone, Jonathan Ross, Jimmy Knapp and Janet Street-Porter, for example.

In the past few years major changes have occurred regarding regional accents. They have become more acceptable and even fashionable. Telephone call centres are manned by Scottish and Yorkshire voices; regional voices are part of our popular culture, with radio and television personalities speaking in accents far removed from received pronunciation. Younger members of the royal family do not sound as if they have stepped out of a 1940s film like *Brief Encounter* and have dropped the clipped vowel sounds of Celia Johnson. Even compare the voice of Queen Elizabeth at her coronation with more recent recordings to hear the changes that have taken place.

Voice coaches who are asked to change a client's voice often find that they only need to change their posture and breathing in order to achieve more clarity.

However, I should issue a word of warning to you if you have a strong regional accent. People whose mother tongue is not English may have difficulty understanding you, so you will need to put on your 'posh' accent for them.

Posture

If you slump in any way, or habitually push your head forwards when you're speaking, your ability to project and vary your voice may be restricted. Try to stand tall, with your feet parallel and roughly hip-bone width apart. This will help to ground you, and check that your head position is centred. It's helpful to do some gentle exercises to ease out tension in your neck and shoulders, such as circling your shoulders slowly backwards a few times, easing your ear down towards your shoulder on each side, looking over each shoulder, dropping your chin down on to your chest, and then gently moving your chin from side to side on your chest before very slowly bringing your head up into a centred position – feeling you're lifting up from your waist, and from behind your ears. If you feel that your posture needs to be improved, try Pilates, yoga or the Alexander technique. It is well worth correcting your posture because bad postural habits don't improve with age!

Volume, Clarity, Variety

To be an effective speaker you need to:

- be heard;
- be understood;
- have variety in your voice.

How to be heard

There are speakers whose soft voices make it difficult for their listeners to hear them, even in a small group. In addition there may be background noise – roadworks and traffic outside in the street, air conditioning or heating noise inside, as well as the general hubbub from adjoining rooms. After a while listeners give up straining to hear the quiet voice of the speaker and indulge in some internal conversations with themselves.

With larger audiences, you may have to speak over the sound of latecomers arriving, or the rattle of china and cutlery, as well as coughing and nose blowing.

The secret of voice projection is to use your breath to support your voice as you speak from the stomach. If you exert pressure on your throat muscles to speak louder, your voice will sound strained and you will end up with a sore throat.

Breathe well to speak well

Most of us don't use our lungs well. In our everyday lives we take short, shallow breaths and only fill the top half of our lungs. Under stress we breathe more rapidly, and because we are not using the full capacity of our lungs, we become breathless; when we are speaking, we can even run out of air before we reach the end of a sentence.

The deeper you breathe, the more air you will have to sustain your voice and project it to all your listeners. It's important to try and get in touch with your abdominal breathing (which is also very calming) by relaxing your shoulders and stomach, placing your hands on your stomach just below the navel, and then starting to notice the gentle rise and fall of the stomach as the breath comes in and out. You get fatter with an inwards breath, slimmer with an outwards one. Practise this first lying on the floor, with a book or cushion to support your head and with your knees bent. Then do it sitting, and finally standing. It's helpful also to put a hand on your ribs to feel their simultaneous upwards and outwards movement, as well as to feel your lower back moving outwards and inwards as you breathe – giving a sense of all-round expansion with as much air as you need for speech.

Now, take a deep breath and count aloud on that one breath. You should reach twenty plus, but don't cheat. Full lungs will enable you to finish long sentences with no ums or ers, and will kill some of your panic and take the strain off your larynx, so that you will be able to project your voice like an opera singer.

Imagine that the air in your lungs is like water coming out of a garden hose; it can dribble out over the lawn or you can place your thumb over the end and direct it to the furthest corners of the garden. When you count out loud, control your air so that you can extend it for longer and longer. Each time you attempt this counting exercise, try to increase your breath control to reach a higher and higher number, and to extend your voice to the far corners of the room and beyond.

Projecting through a wall

Imagine that your voice is a laser beam and it can penetrate the wall into the next room. You will need lots of air to extend it in a controlled jet, past your voice box and unrestricted by your throat muscles and out through your mouth. Practise reading from this book into a tape recorder in your normal voice and then again projecting into the next room. You should be able to hear the difference as you use more air to carry your voice further and further. Remember not to force your voice – use the breath to support it. There is no excuse for not being heard. If you suspect or have been told that you have a soft voice, practise using more air in your everyday conversation. At first it may feel unnatural and too loud, but persevere and you will find that people take more notice of you and interrupt you less. If you develop a strong voice, you will be perceived as someone who is worth listening to and will have no trouble participating at meetings. Don't let your voice drop at the ends of sentences, but maintain the same volume right to the final full stop.

How to be understood

Some people speak with their teeth together, hardly moving their lips, and then wonder why they are not understood. I've said that you should be taking in air and there is no reason to keep it trapped behind your teeth. You don't have to save it. Let it out as you try this exercise. Say the alphabet out loud, opening your mouth wide as if you were talking through a half-yawn, and imagine your jaws cannot close and your lips cannot touch, except on the letters B, M, P and W. Repeat the exercise using twice as much air and projecting into the next room; hold your pen in your hand between your lips to make sure they don't touch.

Try saying these sentences smoothly all on one breath, without pauses or jerkiness:

- 'No man would listen to you talk unless he knew that it was his turn next.'

- 'It is always the best policy to speak the truth, unless you are an exceptionally good liar.'

- 'One of the tests of leadership is the ability to recognise a problem before it becomes an emergency.'

Lost letters and swallowed sounds

Clarity and good diction don't mean changing your accent or personality, but do mean positively pronouncing every letter and sound in order to minimise the risk of being misunderstood. For example, 'Good morning' instead of 'G' morning'; 'little' instead of 'li'le'; and 'part of this market' instead of 'par o' dis mar'e'.

How to add variety

You should aim to add variety to your voice because even if the words of your talk are stimulating, if your voice doesn't sound exciting you will not have credibility and you won't keep your listeners' attention.

Some speakers have a naturally varied voice with plenty of 'colour', while others have to modify their voice consciously to sound more interesting. Nerves can often affect your voice and make it sound more monotone than normal. When assessing your own voice, don't rely only on a tape recorder, as it is difficult to listen objectively to how you sound. Ask colleagues for feedback on whether you need to improve the variety in your voice.

If you want to enliven your voice, you also need to vary:

- volume;

- speed;

- pitch.

You also need to consider inflexion and emphasis (see below).

Volume

We have already looked at how you can learn to project your voice so that it can be heard and so that you sound more authoritative; now consider the power you have to vary the volume. Decrease it if you have an important point you want to emphasise: 'Now, I am going to reveal to you the extent of petty thieving in this school.' Increase it when you call for action: 'We cannot allow this to continue.' Allow yourself to be dramatic and vary your volume to add spice to your voice.

You may feel that this is totally inappropriate behaviour for the small group meetings you attend. Before you dismiss these suggestions, think of some of the men and women whom you consider to be interesting speakers – you'll find that without it being obvious, they are using a wide range of volume when they speak. I'm not proposing that you sound like a great actor playing King Lear or Lady Macbeth, but I am drawing your attention to the importance of *varying* your volume in order to avoid speaking in a dull, flat voice.

Speed

My clients often find that although they time their talks for one of our training room exercises, when they present to the group, they finish too early. This is because nerves affect their delivery and they talk more quickly. Learn to slow down. Speak at half the speed you think is correct and you will be understood better. Your words will be clearer and you will feel more in control. You can add power to your talk by slowing down and using pauses to indicate a change of subject and for emphasis.

Pauses mean power

Remember how difficult it is for the listener to follow the spoken word, and make it easier for them by pausing when you are moving from one point to another. You should slow down between words and between ideas. Novice speakers find pausing one of the most difficult techniques to acquire, but it is a very effective means of holding your audience's attention.

Use the pause to add emphasis to your words: 'We are facing a very difficult period in the history of the organisation [pause] very difficult [pause, and look around with good eye contact], but the solution is here in this room [pause], in your hands.'

Silent pauses

Pauses are powerful only if they are silent. Speakers who can't bear silence fill it with the noise of their brain working as they search for the exact words. When their brain gets into gear, it emits the sound of 'er' and 'um' and 'mm' – non-words that convey nothing and distract listeners. Learn to think silently. Even in your everyday conversation, you may find that you are using other non-words such as 'I mean', 'basically', 'you know', 'actually' and 'you know what I mean', etc., so try to eliminate them completely as they are unnecessary and indicate a lack of concentration on your part. Sharpen up your conversation and eventually you will be sufficiently confident to pause when you are speaking in public.

Earlier in this book, I said that our brains process words at 500 words a minute and listeners can be easily distracted by their own thoughts because you are talking at only 150 words a minute. This difference between brain and speaking speeds works to your advantage when you are searching for a word. What you imagine to be a full half-minute's silence is actually only a second or two, and is totally unnoticed by your audience. Time and time again on our courses, clients see themselves on video and are amazed that 'that terrible silence when I lost myself completely' turns out to be a passing moment. Remember, a pause is a compliment to the audience. You are showing you want to express yourself well and are taking time to choose the right words. No one expects you to be as word perfect as an actor – on the contrary, that might seem insincere – but neither do they want to hear your brain crashing through its gears with 'ers' and 'ums'.

Varying your speed

As well as using pauses, you must learn to change the speed of your delivery to add variety. Giving introductory background information and setting the scene for your subject may contain information with which most of the audience is familiar, so your delivery can be faster than that which you would use when you reach the main thrust of your argument.

When I referred to volume, I mentioned the dramatic effect of speaking more quietly and also of using the full range from loud to soft; this can be combined with speed to make a memorable impact. Use a slow delivery and a low, soft voice (still audible) to capture the audience's attention.

Adding highs and lows

Many speakers find that nerves cause their voice to go up a few notes. Research shows that lower voices are more believable, so if you would like to pitch yours lower you can practise the following exercise. Imagine you have a large Chinese gong and are beating it, bong, bong, bong. Say out aloud the words, 'Chinese gong, Chinese gong, gong, gong, bong, bong.' On each 'ong' sound, elongate the sound so that you can feel the vibrations in your throat. If you practise saying this for two minutes every morning and evening, your voice will be permanently lowered for as long as you keep up the exercise. You can test this out with a tape recorder. Speak into it before doing the exercises and again afterwards and you will hear that your voice has become lower.

However, you need highs as well as lows so that you avoid speaking in a monotone. Allow your voice to go up as you ask rhetorical questions, for example 'How can we show we care?' There is a tendency for some people to use an upwards inflection even when they are stating a fact. Some speech researchers have suggested that this phenomenon is due to the many Australian soap operas on TV. Whatever the reason, be wary of falling into this habit because it gives the impression that you are unsure of yourself and your facts and are looking for corroboration from your listeners.

Inflexion

Here is an opportunity to practise using the full range of your voice by saying the word 'really' to indicate the feelings expressed below:

'I have just lost my job.' 'Really?' (horror)
'You need to get your hair cut.' 'Really.' (annoyance)
'Your work is exceptionally good.' 'Really.' (pleasure)
'We will be finishing on time.' 'Really.' (disbelief)
'Truly I am looking forward to 'Really.' (sarcasm)
  working for him.'

Even a simple word like 'Hello' can indicate a variety of emotions by changing the inflexion.

'Hello' (pleased to see friends)
'Hello' (male welcoming a female friend)
'Hello' (surprised and delighted)

Notice as you say each of these 'Hellos' that the inflexion to show the feeling is always on the vowel sound. Therefore, if you want to give colour to your voice you should e-lon-gate the vowels. Try saying the following sentence: 'I want to stay here for ever and ever' as 'I waaant to staaay heeere for eeeever and eeeever.'

Using Emphasis

Try giving a different meaning to the following sentence by emphasising a different word each time you read it: 'Are you coming with me?' Emphasising the important words in your talk will help the listener and add variety and colour to your voice.

You can enhance the quality of the word, for example 'I am *delighted* to hear your good news,' 'I was so *sorry* to hear he had died.'

With emphasis, you can put energy into your words. Try combining them with pausing. For example, 'He was [pause] a great leader.'

Further Exercises

I have mentioned the components of an interesting voice, but simply reading about them will not improve your delivery.

You need to *practise*. If you do not have the opportunity to practise your speaking in public as much as you would like, or if you prefer to do so outside your own working environment, consider joining a speaking club that offers you the possibility of learning to present your views in an interesting and persuasive manner. Members of most of these clubs come from a variety of backgrounds and attend with the common purpose of practising their speaking skills. Each speaker is assessed following his assignment, a prepared speech or spontaneous talk, say, so that he receives instant feedback on his performance to enable him to improve.

I advise my clients to read aloud. Try reading a book to your children, or read a passage from a newspaper into a tape recorder to learn how to add variety, colour and drama to your voice. To be a convincing speaker, you need the magical quality of enthusiasm. Although it may be bubbling away inside you, if your voice doesn't express it, your audience won't be able to share it with you. For many of us speaking on the phone represents a large part of our 'speaking in public'. Obviously when you are on the phone listeners cannot see you, and it is even more important to use your voice in a positive way to reinforce your message. In advance of important telephone calls consider what you want to achieve and what packaging of your message will be most effective. Do you want to ask a favour? Make a complaint? Urge someone to a course of action? Or do you simply want get some information in the shortest time? The right tone of voice will help you realise your objective.

Just before a presentation it's worth doing some warm-up exercises like actors and singers always do. A presentation can be the equal of a marathon for a voice unused to such pressure; just as people warm up leg muscles for a race, so the muscles creating voice and speech benefit from getting into a fit state for action. If nothing else, just do some gentle humming (sliding your voice up and down your range, within comfort level) and recite a few tongue twisters (see below).

Articulation – the clarity of the words

You should aim to make the consonants clear and precise – consonants carry the meaning of the language, while vowels carry the sound. In order to make the consonants clear the organs making the consonant sounds must be clear and precise in their movements; the organs are lips, tongue and soft palate, in combination with the teeth and hard palate.

Here are some useful exercises to help with clarity:

1. Loosen jaw – draw hands down face and let jaw relax easily.

2. Open and close mouth easily as you repeat FAH FAH FAH FAH. BLAH BLAH.

3. For loosening jaw, say SAH KAH SHE FAH RAH – PAH KAH SHE FAH RAH – WAH KAH SHE FAH RAH – BAH KAH SHE FAH RAH – DAH KAH SHE FAH RAH.

4. For loosening lips, say WWW WWW WWW BBB BBB BBB WBW WBW WBW.

5. For loosening tongue, move tongue tip to behind upper teeth and then to behind lower teeth (keep jaw open and still) – LLD DDD LLL DDD LDL LDL LDL.

6. For combination loosening, say LLL LDL WWW LDL WLWD.

7. Phrases for precise articulation: 'The tip of the tongue, the teeth and the lips,' 'Lah lee bo lee zip e do da,' 'Repetition, repetition, repetition,' 'Whenever the weather is cold, whenever the weather is hot,' 'We'll weather the weather whatever the weather whether we like it or not.'

Variety

Variety in the voice can be achieved by variation in volume, pitch, speed and pause.

These exercises are designed to increase awareness of your own speech rhythm and sound pattern. Speak them aloud, varying your volume, pitch and speed.

EXERCISE 1 **Volume**

Loud, louder, shout, quiet, quietest, whisper, silence.
Crash, bang, clatter, smash. Hush, plush, slush.
Creep, peep, asleep. Hit, bit, grit.

EXERCISE 2 **Pitch**

Centre, high, low, deep, deepest, highest.
Up and down, awake, asleep, sky-high, ocean-deep.

When I sing the note gets higher and higher and higher.
When I speak the pitch gets lower and lower and lower.

In order to avoid a continuing downwards inflection, don't start a sentence on the finishing note of the previous sentence.

EXERCISE 3 **Speed**

Fast, faster, fastest, quick, lightning, flash, slow, slower, cease.
Run, jump, leap, stop, slink, drawl, crawl, elongate, lengthen, hiss, buzz, jab, insinuate, prod, glide, float, dream.
The lion gave a sudden stop.
He let the dainty morsel drop,
And slunk reluctant to his cage,
Snarling with disappointed rage.

EXERCISE 4 **Pause**

Vary the time lapse between the following words:
Start.stop..begin.end....commence...cease..go...stop.resume.....
desist.continue.refrain.

EXERCISE 5 **Reading aloud**

'He came into the room, looked at the disorder and was perplexed. How it came to be like this he could not imagine. The silence was unbroken. He waited anxiously for some sign of life. Nothing at all. His eye moved furtively from wall to door, from floor to . . . corner . . . There in the corner, slumped between overturned chairs was a man, face drained to a pallor, and still as a lifeless creature. There was no phone in the house, no means of contact with the outside world. There was nothing to be done but to leave immediately and run, run as fast as he could away from the disorder, away from the chaos, away from responsibility. Tell no one, tell no one, get away, far away, run, run, fast, faster, faster: feet moving, feet, feet, feet, feet . . . out of step, not my step; step, other step, louder, nearer, quicker, thus, thud. Stop.'

Voice Care

Do:

- drink at least two litres of still water a day;
- inhale steam;
- reduce tea and coffee consumption (caffeine and alcohol are drying agents);
- stop smoking – and avoid smoky atmospheres;
- avoid throat clearing (bite your tongue – gently! – to generate saliva, swallow or take a sip of water);
- rest your voice each day.

Don't:

- force your voice over noise;

- push a tired voice;

- talk or whisper with an infected larynx;

- drink alcohol before speaking – however tempting!

Breathing and voice exercises

Breathing is fundamental to life. Although it is involuntary, most of use less than 10 per cent of our lungs' true capacity. Through deep breathing, we can greatly enhance our vocal performance.

EXERCISE 1   **Vacuuming the lungs** (breathing properly)

Breathe out all the air in your lungs. When you think they are empty, purse your lips and give an extra squeeze from the stomach. Close your mouth and pinch your nostrils together. When you feel blue and think you are about to collapse, simply release your fingers from your nose. Do not open your mouth or try to breathe in any way. Automatically the cold air will hit a spot deep in the pit of your stomach. This is the spot you should aim for when breathing deeply.

EXERCISE 2   **Panting** (build breath endurance)

Take a deep breath, into the spot you identified in Exercise 1. Be careful not to raise the shoulders. Use a mirror to check. Pant like a dog, very lightly. You should be able to feel the top of your diaphragm (the muscle just below your breastbone) quivering in and out as you pant. Sustain it for as long as you can. Try to build gradually to 30 seconds and then 1 minute.

Exercise 3 **Counting by numbers** (breath control)

In this exercise it is important to keep a steady counting rhythm going. If you can borrow a metronome, set it to about 70–80 beats per minute to keep time. Alternatively, this is a good exercise to do while walking outside. Each step is one count. Take a good breath in to a count of four. Count aloud to four, then exhale silently to a count of four. Repeat four times. Breathe in to four, count to eight then exhale over eight beats. Repeat four times. Breathe in to four, count to twelve, exhale to a count of eight. Repeat four times.

Exercise 4 **Choo choo train** (breathing strength)

Take a good breath and hiss loudly until your breath is expelled. Practise hissing in short and long bursts varying the patterns. With practice, see if you can lengthen the exhalation while hissing to 25 or 30 seconds.

Exercise 5 **ha, ha, HA!** (volume)

Choose a point close to you in the room. It could be the corner of a table, or a door handle. Take a good breath and say 'ha' to the point and imagine the sound comes back to you in a straight line. Pick a point further away, say 3 to 4 metres. Say 'HA' to this point in the same way. Finally, concentrate on the furthest point in the room from where you are standing, say 'HA!' in the same way, and 'feel' the sound return to you along the same line it went. Practise this a few times, and you should feel the kick in your diaphragm increase as you say 'ha' each time. Keep going until you can definitely feel the difference in the volume you need to hit each point.

Exercise 6 **One to ten** (voice projection)

Take a good breath. Count to ten aloud, slowly, starting in a whisper and building up the volume so that it is loudest when you reach ten. Repeat, but be careful that the pitch (level) of the voice does not rise as you get louder. Concentrate on keeping it at the same level as the volume increases.

EXERCISE 7   **Hickory dicotry** (lowering a high voice)

This one is good for lowering high voices (particularly female), which tend to be worse when we are nervous. Stand up straight and take a good breath. Start saying the nursery rhyme 'Hickory Dickory Dock', bending forwards from the waist as you do so. You should be bent over so that your upper body is parallel to the floor as you reach the word 'clock' and you should notice a slight drop in pitch. Continue the rhyme and unbend as you do so, listening carefully so as not to let the pitch slip up again. Now repeat the rhyme in this lower pitch, without bending over. Try with other nursery rhymes for variation!

EXERCISE 8   **The bells** (varying tone)

Stand tall and take a good breath. Say (in a sing-song voice) 'bing bong' in the highest voice you can, immediately followed by 'ding dong' in a medium-pitched voice, and then 'king kong' in the lowest voice possible. As you do so, put your right hand above your head, at shoulder height and then dropped down by your side respectively. Repeat until the changes between the registers are smooth.

EXERCISE 9   **Roller-coaster** (varying pitch)

Say nursery rhymes (or any sentences) aloud as if you are creating a roller-coaster with your voice. Go from high to low in sweeping movements, and practise different words on different pitches each time. Do this for about 2 minutes at a time, rest for 1 minute, then repeat.

EXERCISE 10 **The articulators** (clear articulation)

Say in a clear voice, 'The tip of the tongue, the teeth and the lips.' These are what we call the articulators. They form the consonants that make our words understandable. Make sure when you say this sentence that you pay particular attention to the 'd' of the 'and'. Practise at varying speeds and different volumes.

EXERCISE 11 **Tongue twisters** (improving articulation)

Say your favourite tongue twisters, concentrating on the ones you find the most difficult. Start slowly and build up speed. Practise at different volumes, paying special attention to the consonants at the ends of words. Here are a few to start you off:

A flea and fly got lost in a flute, said the fly let us flee, said the flea let us fly, so they flew through a flaw in the flute.

Red leather, yellow leather. (Repeat six times.)

Peter Piper picked a peck of pickled peppers. If Peter Piper picked a peck of pickled peppers, where's the peck of pickled peppers Peter Piper picked?

A proper cup of coffee in a proper copper coffee pot.

SUMMARY

- Breath will give authority to your voice.
- Opening your mouth will make you easier to understand.
- Try to vary the volume, speed and pitch.
- Silent pauses are powerful and enable your listeners to assess what you are saying.

13

Using Humour

'Wit had truth in it; wisecracking is simply
callisthenics with words.'
DOROTHY PARKER

Now that you're feeling more sure of yourself and have estab-
lished your voice, I'd like to look at the reasons for using
humour and how to do it effectively. I have to admit that I
debated whether or not to write this chapter, because I find the
subject of humour difficult. However, I suspect that you may
feel the same and, for that reason, I am including a few suggestions on how to make your audience smile. The humour I am
describing isn't intended to provoke helpless laughter in your
audience. If you *are* able to achieve this and you feel it appropriate for your situation you won't need to read the rest of this
chapter. Alternatively, you may feel uneasy about attempting
to be funny and you may worry that you will run the risk of
ruining a good talk by including what turns out to be an
unamusing witticism. If you feel like this, remember that there
is no obligation to be humorous. But, if you can do it successfully, there are several advantages.

Why Include Humour?

Humour relaxes the audience and also eases the tension for you. Audiences, even a small group, sense the apprehension you feel as you stand to speak to them and they want to be reassured that they are in good hands. By giving them something to laugh at, you show that you are in control. Smiling and laughing together unites an audience and creates an atmosphere of listening together. An audience of local business people enjoyed this comment from a bank manager: 'It seems to me that many people look on a visit to their bank manager with the same dread as a visit to the dentist. Really we're not that bad.' You can establish a rapport with the audience by using humour so that they feel well disposed towards you, which is particularly important if you are selling ideas or products.

Humour is useful to lighten a heavy and possibly dull passage in your talk and to make it more digestible and therefore more memorable. Take a look at your own experience, your own background and the subject area you're talking about to find stories that are funny and prompt a small smile of recognition on people's faces. You can also use humour to illustrate major points or the transition between them.

Humour for Business Presentations

The humour that is suitable for a business presentation is difficult to classify, but it may be helpful to describe what it is not. Jokes are risky because they require a positive reaction from the audience, and if it's not forthcoming, it is obvious that the joke has flopped. A joke that fails to raise a smile causes embarrassment for you and for the audience, and has the opposite effect to the one that you intended. Professional comedians will tell you that audiences vary enormously and a joke that was successful one night may not even raise a titter on another. Ask yourself if you can afford to misjudge what will be an acceptable joke for your audience. Even when your joke is pertinent, you may ruin its effect by incorrect timing, emphasising the wrong word or, worse still, getting the punchline muddled up. You may be a proficient joke teller within your group of friends, but it takes a special talent to deliver a joke successfully to larger audiences. There are other ways of including humour in your talk which don't require such a positive and therefore obvious reaction from the audience, and which, if unsuccessful, will not cause embarrassment to you or the audience.

The safest target for your humour is yourself. Show them your weaknesses and admit your failings. Tell stories against yourself. For instance, I remember the occasion when, as a guest speaker at a luncheon, I was waiting to be introduced. The chairman turned to me and asked if I was ready to begin and unfortunately added, 'Or shall we allow them to enjoy themselves a little longer?'

You may find that some of the best humour arises out of the situation, so don't be self-conscious about voicing a comment if it springs to mind. But never use the words, 'That reminds me of a story about ...' because the tale that follows is usually irrelevant.

If you intend using humour in your talk to make people smile, you must know how to identify shared experiences and problems. Your humour must be relevant to the audience and should help to show that you are one of them or that you understand their situation and are in sympathy with their point of view. Depending on whom you are addressing, the problems will be different. If you are talking to a group of managers, you may refer to the disorganised methods of their secretaries; alternatively, if you are addressing secretaries, you may want to comment on their disorganised bosses. A management audience will probably respond to a witty remark about coping with difficult staff and an audience of staff members will appreciate a remark criticising management.

Here is an example, which I heard at a nurses' convention,

of a story that worked well because the audience all shared the same view of doctors. A man arrives in heaven and is being shown around by St Peter. He sees wonderful accommodation, beautiful gardens, sunny weather, and so on. Everyone is very peaceful, polite and friendly until, waiting in a queue for lunch, the new arrival is suddenly pushed aside by a man in a white coat, who rushes to the head of the line, grabs his food and stomps over to a table by himself. 'Who is that?' the new arrival asked St Peter. 'Oh, that's God,' came the reply, 'but sometimes he thinks he's a doctor!'

If you are part of the group you are addressing, you will be in a position to know the experiences and problems that are common to all of you, and it will be appropriate for you to make a passing remark about the inedible canteen food or the chairman's notorious bad taste in ties. With other audiences you mustn't attempt to gatecrash with humour, as they will resent an outsider making disparaging remarks about their canteen or their chairman. You will be on safer ground if you stick to scapegoats like the Post Office, poor service from garages and banks, and the vagaries of the weather.

If you feel awkward being humorous, you must practise aloud so that it becomes more natural. Include a few casual and apparently off-the-cuff remarks that you can deliver in a relaxed and unforced manner. Often it's the delivery and timing that causes the audience to smile, so speak slowly and remember that a raised eyebrow or a quizzical look may help to show that you are making a light-hearted remark.

Look for the humour. It often comes from the unexpected, such as twist on a familiar quote – 'If at first you don't succeed, give up', 'The darkest hour is just before you're overdrawn', or a play on words or on a situation. Search for exaggeration and understatements. Look at your talk and pick out a few words or sentences that you can turn about and inject with humour. In a serious presentation, an unexpected colloquial expression adds a light note – for instance, 'an almighty cock-up' instead of 'a significant error'.

You'll also find humour in your everyday life. Look back to yesterday and you'll remember something that may not have seemed particularly funny at the time, but that would be so in retelling.

Humour for Social Events

It is unlikely that you can be amusing for an entire five or ten minutes so unless you are extremely gifted don't attempt to deliver a speech that relies entirely on humour. The humour will also be more appreciated if you have some quieter moments between the laughs.

It's important for your humour to fit the subject and, as in all presentations, you need to thoroughly understand the audience. When humour backfires it's usually because the speaker is not using it properly. Jokes can be inappropriate because they are insulting, stupid or not relevant to the audience, and some of the most dangerous topics are race, sex, religion, politics, handicaps and sexual orientation. Humour succeeds where there is a shared frame of reference, and you can make those on the outside the butt of the joke, for instance a competing sports team or local councillors who're increasing parking fees, or women (for an all-male audience) or men (for an all-female group), or parents (when the audience consists of teenagers) or teenagers (for an audience of parents).

Build a Humour File

There are several books available purporting to contain humour and wit. I have listened to highly amusing speakers who have incorporated stories and anecdotes in their talks, which I know to have originated from these sources, but I think it takes a particularly discerning eye to recognise a funny story in print. The secret of employing what I call 'second-hand humour' is to personalise it so that it appears to be your own experience. Here's an example:

> A young man who was just about to embark on a business career went to see his grandfather, who had founded the family firm. 'Remember, my boy, that in business honesty is still the best policy.'
>
> 'Right, grandfather,' said the grandson.
>
> 'But before you do anything else, read up on company law,' recommended the old man. 'You would be surprised at the kinds of thing that you can do in the name of business and still be honest.'

You can modify this story by recalling the advice that your own father gave you when you started work: 'He told me that in business honesty is the best policy. He also advised me to read up on company law because, as he put it, "You'd be surprised at the kinds of thing you can do in the name of business and still be honest."'

Reading this story now you'll probably not find it particularly amusing, but remember that in the right context and with the appropriate audience it will provide a light-hearted moment.

If you are talking to a group of people you know well, you can substitute the name of a mutual colleague in order to personalise the story: 'I understand that Adam Sums, our new accountant, was asked by the managing director during his interview, "What is ten times ten?" Apparently he made his mark by replying, "That rather depends on the figure you had in mind, sir."'

Looking through books of humour is time-consuming and should only be undertaken in small chunks, as after a while nothing seems to be amusing. Try putting such books by the side of the lavatory or by your bed so that you can read a few stories at a time and judge them individually.

Keep a cuttings file of news about your region, town, industry or profession. You may find that you can link several incidents into a humorous story. Steal other people's ideas and anecdotes if they help to illustrate your point of view.

Keep a file of case histories, examples and stories you have found funny and feel you'll be able to use in future. You'll only be able to use it if you keep track of it. Ideas just fly away if you don't capture them on paper in such a way that you can find them when you need them.

Watch television programmes and crib from them. Many scripts are now available in book form and some one-liners are useful to add a sparkle to your talk. But be careful only to use material that is relevant to the audience. Also beware of sexist stories that will antagonise women, and avoid religious and racist comments.

If you do use material from a well-known personality you can preface your remarks by using his or her name. For example, 'On the subject of politicians, I agree with Clive Anderson when he said that they have a lot in common with chimpanzees – the higher they climb the more unpleasant features they reveal.' Incidentally this is a story that can be adapted to suit any audience or group of people by substituting the appropriate word for politicians. Here is another example, 'Bob Hope put it well when he described banks as places that will lend you money only if you can prove that you don't need it.'

How to Deliver a Humorous Line

Humour should never be announced: 'I must tell you an amusing thing my father said to me ...' This kills the story. Your wit must appear to be a spontaneous throwaway comment that the audience can choose to smile at. If you tell them beforehand that they will find it funny, they will be expecting an exceptionally good story. Unannounced humour makes the audience feel that they have individually recognised the fun side of your character. It's the difference between having a good meal in an unknown restaurant that you have personally discovered and having a good meal in a highly recommended restaurant. The first meal will be unexpected and therefore will seem better, even if it is not. The most successful humour is the unexpected peep behind the serious exterior. Your delivery mustn't indicate that you are telling an amusing story. A twinkle in your eye is more appealing than laughter and giggles at your own witticisms. Remember to slow down for the punchline and be careful to enunciate every word.

Beware of relying on an accent, dialect or funny voice to be amusing – you may find it difficult to reproduce it accurately under stress.

Never read anecdotes, humorous stories or jokes, as they'll sound artificial and forced. Your humour should appear to be spontaneous and uncontrived, and you can't achieve this naturalness if you are reading every word. You also need plenty of eye contact to judge how your humour is being received.

Timing is crucial if your humour is to succeed. This is a combination of pausing between words and sentences, and phrasing, which is grouping words together. Record one of your favourite comedians and analyse how he or she uses pauses effectively. Try to stress the important words. Pause after your humorous line, but quickly pick up the thread of your talk after the audience has reacted. If there is no response, don't agonise, simply continue in a calm, unruffled manner. Some of the audience may be smiling inside. You are not a comic and the success of your presentation doesn't depend on your ability to bring the house down. I know from experience that different audiences can respond differently to the same line and, if an expected smile doesn't materialise, you must carry on with the rest of your talk. I prefer to stick to one-liners because they can pass unnoticed if they don't succeed, and not throw you off course.

Inexperienced speakers will often swallow or mumble humorous remarks because they are concerned that they won't be considered funny by the audience. That's a sure-fire path to failure. Don't include humour if you feel uncomfortable about speaking out. You need courage and confidence to win a round of smiles.

Like all speaking, your humour must be researched and practised until you feel comfortable and familiar with it. Your body language and facial expressions, as well as your timing, are most important. Memorise your humorous lines so that you can look at your audience. Witty, light-hearted comments that are self-deprecating or which knock a common enemy are more effective than long, elaborate jokes. Aim to tickle the audience's mind.

SUMMARY

- Remember that humour unites audiences.

- Try to identify and use common problems and shared experiences.

- You are most likely to fail if you tell complicated jokes.

- You could start by collecting funny stories.

- Humour must be delivered directly to the listeners so never read your humorous lines.

- If you aim for chuckles, not belly laughs, you are most likely to succeed.

14

Handling Questions Convincingly

'That's a good question for you to ask, not a wise question
for me to answer.'
ANTHONY EDEN (to reporter in 1953, when asked what effect Stalin's
death might have on international affairs)

'Be sincere; be brief; be seated.'
FRANKLIN D. ROOSEVELT

You've now carefully thought through your talk or presentation – how you will look, what to say, how to say it, whether
to use anecdotes, quotes or humour. But it is also important to
prepare for what might happen at the end.

Few presenters can get away without answering questions
from their audience. You may even want to encourage an
interactive style so that questions are asked and answered as
they occur. You may be in a situation where you will be asked
many questions, for example at a job interview or in a small
group, which is more discussion-based than a formal presentation.

Some speakers dread questions as they imagine they will be
challenged and made to look foolish. There is only one way to
prevent this from happening – anticipate and prepare. In this

chapter I describe ideas you can use in order to continue to project a confident presence as you answer questions.

When to Allow Questions

In small groups you may decide to answer questions throughout your talk, as they occur naturally when they are most relevant. It's also a good idea to encourage questions if you are presenting an instructional talk as you'll need to check comprehension – and questions can provide valuable feedback for you.

I said earlier in this book that I prefer to ask for questions to be kept until the end of my talk so that I can present my material in the order I have chosen, but when I am running training classes, I often pause for questions. In fact, I involve participants by asking them questions as much as possible (see Chapter 18 on interacting with your audience). This helps to maintain a higher level of concentration and allows the listeners to become active participants; questions also enable me to check that everyone has understood.

There are disadvantages to allowing questions during your presentation:

- they could disrupt the flow and structure of your talk;

- the answer may be contained later on in your talk;

- only one person may be interested, i.e. the questioner.

If you decide to take questions as they occur be sure to indicate to the rest of the group where the answer fits into the overall plan of your talk – for example, 'David's question opens up the area of whose responsibility it is to check the fire alarm each month. I will answer that and then come back to the main theme of office security.'

You may be able to control a spontaneous question-and-answer session in a small informal group, but large audiences need to be managed more firmly. If you are the sole speaker, let the audience know when you expect questions and even suggest to them that they jot down those that occur to them as you are talking.

You should always schedule your questions before your final summing up so that you can end on a positive note. Don't forget that your last words to the audience will be retained longest and you don't want these to be a minor argument that you had with a questioner. When question time is over, if you have been unlucky enough to face any difficult or hostile questions, you should regain control by repeating your main points. Demonstrate to the audience that you are a reasonable person by finishing on a humorous note if this is appropriate.

When you restate your main proposition, include any comments from others present who support it and ignore adverse questions or remarks. Thus, you show that you are confident and can cope calmly with controversy. Listeners don't want to see you embarrassed and they expect you to behave in a professional manner.

If you are introduced by a chairperson, be sure to check beforehand who will handle the question-and-answer session. Unless you are part of a panel discussion, my preference is for the speaker to select the questioners and control the session.

Questions to a Panel

On a panel it's advisable to allow questions immediately after each speaker, because if the audience has to wait until all the speakers have spoken, they will probably only be able to think of questions for the final speaker while the rest of the panel sits there looking superfluous. This happened to me at a conference where not a single question was directed to me, as I had spoken after lunch and the panel discussion was scheduled for the late afternoon. When the chairperson finally took pity on me and redirected a question, I was unable to answer as it was not within my field of experience. Panel questions are valuable, provided that the individual speakers have also had the opportunity to answer questions on their subjects directly after their own talks.

How to Encourage Questions and Avoid Silence

- Tell the audience in advance when you expect questions, i.e. during or at the end of your talk.

- Suggest that they jot down their questions during the talk so that they do not forget them.

- Remember that they need time, at least thirty seconds, to change gear from being passive listeners to active participants.

- Plant a colleague in the audience to ask a relevant question.

- Ask a question yourself. 'You may be wondering why my charity has come to specialise in this area; let me tell you ...' or 'I am sometimes asked about my personal background and you may be interested to know ...'

- Ask the group a question. 'Do you disagree with the area of my talk dealing with the advertising budget, as I know that it is a contentious issue' or 'By a show of hands, could you indicate how many of you have used our services in the past?' Then direct a question to someone: 'Would you care to tell us of your experience, sir?'

Too often speakers cannot tolerate the silence that follows when they ask for questions and they don't allow sufficient time for the audience to respond. Your body language should be alert and interested, but you can indicate that you consider the ball to be in their court by leaning back, maybe sipping some water and adopting a non-threatening listening stance. Above all, don't look anxious.

Rehearsing Questions and Answers

You will find it useful to work out in advance the questions that you may be asked. In fact, try and identify at least six questions that you would hate to be asked. It's an effective policy to anticipate those difficult questions before the event so that you can carefully plan your response. You may wish to enlist the help of other people if you feel you are on shaky ground.

The question-and-answer session should also be rehearsed. There are some obvious advantages; practising helps you to:

• field difficult questions;

• highlight weaknesses in your argument;

• expose potential ambiguity;

• answer questions using additional data;

• handle the unexpected.

How to rehearse

When you are closely involved with a subject, it's possible to arrive at a point where you are talking in your own shorthand and not fully explaining the logic of your arguments. This can be a particular danger when you are an expert talking to a 'lay' audience. Rehearsing your talk in front of colleagues and friends, and asking them to probe any areas that are not completely clear, will help you to avoid this pitfall. If your actual audience has a high level of technical knowledge, try to find someone with a similar degree of understanding of the subject with whom you can rehearse.

When questions arise during your rehearsal period, analyse them and the reason why they have been posed. Is the question:

- relevant and realistic – would your actual audience be likely to ask it?

- referring to material that appears later in your talk?

- one that you want to practise answering for the question-and-answer session.

Ask yourself whether these questions have arisen because of a lack of clarity, too much detail or an illogical argument, or simply because it is impossible to include everything and such a question can be answered at the end of your talk.

Often you can hint in your talk that you will explain further if anyone asks you to do so at the end of your talk: 'As you know we decided not to increase our tours to the US this year and if anyone would like me to explain further about the reasons for this, please ask me at the end of my presentation.'

When you have discovered most of the areas you think may provoke questions, prepare your answers carefully, including additional research into data you may not have had time for in your talk. You will feel more confident if you know that you have fresh, supplementary material to support your case. Be sure to take it with you in a form that is easily accessible during what may be a stressful time. You don't want to be seen shuffling through several files in your briefcase muttering, 'I am sure I had it here somewhere . . .' If you are speaking to a small group, consider preparing an extra handout that outlines the additional evidence.

Look back to your mind map and re-evaluate some of the points you had to reject because of time constraints – might they form the basis of a question-and-answer session?

You may have omitted complex financial figures or technical analyses from your talk as they were inappropriate for the audience – however, a question may require you to provide more exact information.

Listen to the questions

Many inexperienced speakers find it difficult or impossible to handle questions because they fail to do one simple thing – they fail to listen to the question. Therefore remember these points:

- Listen to the question – be sure that you understand it and, if not, ask the questioner to repeat or explain it. This is particularly important in an interview.

- Make notes of the main points of the question if it appears to be multi-layered.

- In a large group ask for the questioner's name (and organisation if it's a public meeting), so that you can refer to them by name.

- Restate the question – this helps you and the rest of the audience to know what question you intend to answer. It is also useful when the acoustics are not good or when the questioner has rambled.

- Answer the question concisely – give your answer directly and, if necessary, supply statistics or use an illustration or even a personal experience to support it. Your audience has heard your speech, so don't give them another; make sure your answer is succinct. In an interview you can ask if they would like you to expand on your answer or give an example of your practical experience in that area.

Some Question and Answer Don'ts

- Don't be defensive. It's easy to feel that the questioner is your adversary, particularly when your subject is controversial. In a public meeting stay calm and polite as you acknowledge the questioner – 'I am sure that many people will be glad you asked that question . . .'

- Don't rush to answer the question. In all situations allow a pause as you consider the full implication of the question and how you can best answer it.

- Don't bluff. If you don't know the answer, say so (see below).

- Don't embarrass the questioner. 'I've already answered that but maybe you weren't listening.' Instead say something like, 'I'm sorry I didn't explain that clearly.'

- Don't get into a dialogue with one questioner. If she insists on asking a supplementary question, answer it briefly and then break eye contact. Look towards the other side of the table or hall and indicate that there is another question. Suggest that, as there are several more questioners, you could discuss her question in more detail after your talk. If a senior manager is monopolising question time, you can ask him if you could answer other questioners and return to him afterwards. Aim to stay in control of the situation. (Also see 'How to Stop Ramblers' below.)

- Don't answer questions that aren't relevant or interesting to all of the listeners. I have witnessed a tax expert who was giving general information on taxation for small businesses become embroiled in a detailed question from one member of the group. He should have suggested that it was inappropriate to discuss one individual case, instead of attempting to answer a personal question that was more suitable for a private discussion.

What to Say if You Don't Know the Answer

No one likes to admit their ignorance and if you are the authority who has just presented a successful talk, it is even more difficult. I am afraid you are going to have to bite the bullet. To help you, imagine that there is someone in the audience who is longing to expose your weakness. So far your presentation has been excellent, but suddenly he hears you giving wrong information – you are bluffing – up he jumps, at last he has caught you!

What can you do if you can't answer a question? Simply admit you don't know, and say you will find out and give the questioner the information when you have had time to do the necessary research. (If it is a large meeting, ask the questioner to leave their name and telephone number with the chairperson.) Sometimes you can use the audience. Ask if anyone has had experience that could help the questioner. You can learn a great deal from the audience, and occasionally it won't be necessary to admit you don't know the answer. This is particularly useful in small groups.

I had a client whose boss delighted in throwing impossible questions at him at their monthly departmental meeting. My client was made to feel inadequate in front of his staff as he attempted to answer. We advised him to face his boss and ask him what questions he needed to prepare for the meeting. This worked for a time until an unexpected question came flying across the room, but fortunately he felt courageous enough to say he didn't know as he hadn't prepared and that it required a detailed answer as it was such an expert question. From then on our client's boss seemed to have fewer questions.

How to Answer Difficult Questions

Hypothetical questions

They are generally prefixed with the words 'What *if* ...' – 'So what happens if the new budget isn't approved?' Don't let yourself be drawn into 'doomsday' situations. Instead answer: 'We've spent two months preparing the new budget. It's a good budget and we're confident we'll get approval to put it into practice.' Politicians generally refuse to answer such questions and you can follow their example by saying that there is too much supposition in the question for you to give a sound answer.

Leading/loaded questions

'Surely you can see how unfair it is for the staff if we close the canteen during August? Why are you insisting on this?' If you don't challenge this first statement, it will appear that you agree with it. 'Everyone knows that this company is making vast profits, so what we want to know is why can't we have one more computer so that the work can be completed faster?' Remember once again to correct the first statement before you answer the question. 'I'd like to know why you think this company is making vast profits.' Here is another example: 'We know that you have found it difficult as the only woman on the board, dear, but do you feel you have achieved anything in your first year?' Don't be tempted to rise to the bait by saying, 'Yes, I have found it very difficult and principally due to your pompous chauvinistic attitude.' Instead you need to change the word 'difficult'. 'Before I answer your question, may I just correct you on one point. I wouldn't describe my first year as difficult. I have found it stimulating and challenging, but above all very enjoyable.'

The yes or no questions

These can appear to be very aggressive. 'Just answer yes or no. Are you going to support me?' You don't have to limit your answer to yes or no – respond in your own words. 'I have considered this issue from three angles and I think you should know what they are. First . . .'

'No win' questions

'Can you explain the decline in your work – is it due to lack of commitment or poor timekeeping or both?' Don't feel you must answer such a question with an 'either/or' answer. You could say: 'I don't think we should look at it in such black and white terms as there are a number of important contributory factors.'

Useful Phrases

The cliché 'I am glad you asked me that' enables you to gain thinking time and you should develop a few more original phrases to help you organise your thoughts before and even during your answer. Here are some suggestions:

- 'To help me answer your question more accurately, could you tell me exactly why you are asking it?'

- 'I can see that you feel strongly about that and I admire you for saying so.'

Sometimes you will not want to answer a question, so you should think about how you can deflect it:

- 'We have spent some time on that problem/question, but what I think is more relevant to consider now is . . .'

- 'There is some merit in those points and it has been useful to hear from you but perhaps you are not aware that ...'

How to Stop Ramblers

On occasion, you'll find that a questioner is unable to pose a question successfully and instead presents a long-winded, rambling speech. What can you do?

- Use body language – hold up your hand and indicate that you want to answer the question if there is one. If not, simply give a brisk thank you and move on to another questioner.

- Highlight one part of the ramble and rephrase it in order to give a short answer.

- Use your voice to interrupt while explaining that time is running out and you can see that there are several other people who wish to ask questions.

These suggestions should be used with caution, depending on your relationship with the questioner.

Handling Hecklers

Sometimes I am asked by a participant on a training course for techniques to handle hecklers. I think it's unlikely that you will be heckled unless you are addressing a public meeting over a controversial issue, but just in case here are a few suggestions:

- Ignore the heckler and look in the opposite direction.

- Do *not* engage in a discussion with the heckler.

- Remember, the audience wants to hear you and is probably feeling embarrassed.

- Use a one-liner slowly and loudly; for example, 'It's good to hear your voice is working well – shame it's not connected to your brain' or 'Now there's a man with a ready wit [turn to the heckler] – do let us know when it is ready.'

I hope that you won't find yourself in a situation where you will need to use any of these techniques.

Your Body Language During Question Time

Your positive, confident stance shouldn't disappear when you stop talking and start taking questions. Listen intently to the question and, even if you think the questioner has totally failed to understand your argument, look pleasant.

As you begin to answer the questioner, look at him directly. However, if it's a fairly involved reply, look around and make eye contact with the rest of the group and include them in your comments. You can also use expressions like, 'I know this applies to many of you . . .' or 'I expect you'll find this useful . . .' so that they don't feel excluded. If you see that some people are nodding or appear to want more explanation, you can extend your answer after asking, 'I can see several of you nodding. Is this a problem that some of you have had to tackle already?'

If you feel under attack, don't allow your body language to reveal your unease – continue to look pleasant and confident as you search in your mind for suitable counter-arguments. I once saw a colleague being given a tough grilling so that afterwards he felt thoroughly exhausted. When I commented on how he had appeared confident and in total control, he said, 'But you couldn't see my pounding heart.' He was right. Don't let yours show either – people take you at face value, so keep looking poised.

SUMMARY

- If you announce when you will answer questions, i.e. during or at the end of your talk, it reminds your listeners that they can ask questions.

- Make sure you have a fall-back technique if there are no questions.

- Anticipate potential questions and rehearse your answers.

- Don't bluff – admit ignorance, even if it is painful to do so.

- Use positive, pleasant body language, especially when you feel under attack.

15

Reducing the Possibility of Disaster

'The more I practise the luckier I get.'
GARY PLAYER

There is no shortcut to success and some experts recommend one hour of preparation for every minute of presentation. Before you throw up your hands in horror, remember that this includes your planning, organising and developing stages as well as the practice.

No one ever allows enough time to practise and some of my clients have a number of wonderful excuses why this should be so: 'The information for the presentation was only ready the night before,' 'If I rehearse I get stale and lack enthusiasm,' 'I know the material inside out,' 'I don't want to look too slick,' and so on ad infinitum.

From my many years' experience of watching speakers, as well as from presenting my own speeches, I know that rehearsing helps you to:

- become familiar with the flow of your material;

- conquer the blank mind syndrome;

- feel more confident and control nerves;

- develop an effective speaking voice;

- use positive and appropriate body language.

You are probably aware that practising is important and yet you keep putting it off until it is too late. I admit that I sometimes do the same and afterwards, when I have finished a presentation, I always wish that I had rehearsed more, because I know that I could have done it better. In reality, when you don't practise, you are using the audience as your rehearsal and that's not fair on them. You are not being fair on yourself either. You've probably spent sufficient time planning the content and choosing the words, but you fail to allocate enough time to what will make the difference between a mediocre and a memorable talk – practice. Remember, if you can get up an hour earlier you gain an extra hour in which to practise.

The Three-step Approach

Take it one step at a time – practice, rehearsal and dress rehearsal. Practising is done by yourself, rehearsing is carried out in front of one or several people, while a dress rehearsal takes place on site with props. All your practising and rehearsing should be spoken aloud, even though you might feel silly. You'll feel worse than silly if you mess up in front of an audience.

Guidelines

Your first run-through will probably help you to add examples and even anecdotes that you hadn't thought of in your original preparation. I find that speaking out loud, even to an empty room, frees the brain to be more creative and so, although I have a full talk prepared at my first practice, I stop and make notes and amendments. Also, if you are reading your speech aloud for the first time, you may find that some sentences are too long or complicated, your choice of words may sound clumsy or you may feel some ideas could be expressed more clearly. It's tempting to continue to alter words and phrases throughout your rehearsing. You must set yourself a time limit for changes, otherwise you will always be rehearsing new material and the main purpose of your practice, to become familiar with your talk, will never be achieved.

Don't forget your body language

You're practising to familiarise yourself with the ideas in your talk and words that convey them; you are also practising your body language and your voice.

Try to stand when you are practising, so that you can use gestures and become used to holding your cards, if you are using them, or advancing your slides on the laptop. This will help you to integrate them into your talk so that it begins to feel like a continuous flow. Look around the room as if you were making eye contact with the audience. Some people like to use a full-length mirror at this stage, but I find it distracting, although there is nothing to beat recording yourself on video. If you don't have your own camera it is possible to hire one; this would be a good investment if you had an important presentation, on which your reputation and that of your organisation rested.

I know of one woman who changed her entire presentation after seeing herself on video because she realised that she was not conveying her message effectively. As she had begun practising well in advance of her 'performance' she had adequate time to do so: another reason for beginning your practice in plenty of time.

Using a tape recorder

If you can't video yourself, the next best thing is to record yourself on a tape recorder. Listen critically to your voice. Is it clear? Are you varying the pitch, volume and speed? Are you using powerful silent pauses or filling up the spaces with non-words? Above all, is there enthusiasm and vitality in your voice? Does it sound interesting? If not, analyse how you can improve it and practise again and again.

If you know that you will be addressing a large audience without the help of a microphone, place your tape recorder at the far side of the room and project your voice to it. Forget your inhibitions and your neighbours. Who cares if they think that your behaviour is strange; it's more important that you practise now and get it right, than worry about the neighbours and later make a fool of yourself in front of a hundred people. Make sure you are not straining your voice. Remember that if your lungs are full of air, your voice will carry further and you won't need to force it.

Rehearsing with feedback

At the stage when you can refine your talk or presentation, a live audience is very useful. Use colleagues or friends, but be sure to give them the context to your talk – who the audience is, what they expect, what your objective is and what you hope to achieve. Only then can your rehearsal audience criticise your talk constructively. You will probably feel very self-conscious and embarrassed but don't give up. Try to give your talk as if you had the actual audience in front of you. Make eye contact, use gestures and sound enthusiastic. Make sure they know that you want them to take the situation seriously and that it is important for you to have this opportunity to practise. If you lose your place, don't make any comment, simply continue as you would in front of a real audience; this will give you practice in overcoming fluffs. Encourage your rehearsal audience to ask questions as this will also be good practice for you (see Chapter 14 on handling questions convincingly). They may want additional information on some aspect of your talk – if so, maybe your real audience would also benefit from an expanded explanation.

When you eventually receive their comments, accept them objectively. It's too easy to say, 'Yes, but ...' and make excuses for not listening to their views. Make notes of what is said to you and only look at them the following day, when there is less pressure on you and you can evaluate them dispassionately.

Remember that to profit from feedback you must accept criticism with an open mind. It may be irritating but consider what an oyster does with a grain of sand – you too can benefit from unpleasant criticism and use it to create a better talk. If you gather enough feedback, you'll end up with a valuable string of pearls.

Be sure to ask your audience to give you positive feedback as well. Not general praise, but specific instances of good performance – you need to know what to keep as well as what to change. In our courses, we insist that our tutors limit their recommendations to a maximum of three points at each feedback session otherwise the students are overwhelmed and unable to assimilate the training.

Guidelines for feedback

These are some questions your rehearsal audience can use in order to assess whether or not you are presenting a successful talk. You may want to add some of your own which are more pertinent or relevant to your subject matter and objective. You can also use this checklist to evaluate your own talk.

Introduction

- Is the first sentence attention grabbing? Does it encourage your audience to want to listen. Sometimes you can pose an apparent contradiction, for example 'I come to bury Caesar: not to praise him.'

- Have you described what your audience will get out of listening to you? Example: 'I intend to give you sufficient information so that by the end of the evening you can decide whether we should go to Paris or Rome.'

- Have you shown why you are qualified to speak on this subject? Example: 'I have known the groom since we were in love with the same girl in kindergarten.'

- Have you announced your structure? Example: 'I propose to give you three reasons why I think that fees should be increased.'

- Have you revealed understanding and knowledge of the listeners' attitudes and possible problems in the first minute or two? Example: 'You may have come here because you distrust the selection process and you'd like to know what safeguards are in place.'

- Have you identified with the audience early on? Example: 'My child is in this school too and I want the best for her; the same as you want for your children.'

Body of talk (some of the following points will not apply to a social speech – you will have to choose what is appropriate for you)

- Have you announced your first point clearly?

- Have you used facts, examples, anecdotes, comparisons and statistics to support your main points?

- Have you summarised regularly?

- Have you recapped on the previous point before moving on to the next one?

- Have you used rhetorical questions to guide your audience along your path?

- Have you avoided jargon and abbreviations?

- Have you used visual aids in order to explain complex material or to add interest at a dull moment?

- Are the links between each point clear and logical?

Conclusion

- Have you indicated that the end of your talk is coming? Example: 'Well, that's all I have to say on my main points.'

- Have you summarised your key points? Example: 'In conclusion, we can increase the budget to ensure an improved service or remain as we are and suffer the consequences.'

- Have you asked for action? Example: 'Do have a look at the samples at the back of the room and remember if you order today there is a 20 per cent discount off everything.'

- Have you ended on a high note? Example: 'Finally, I'd ask you all to raise your glasses and drink to Joe's long and happy retirement.'

Check your timing

Always time every practice so that you know whether you need to add or amend your talk. If you overrun on time, avoid what so many inexperienced speakers do – either ignore it and continue to the end of the talk or speak faster in order to include every precious point. Running over is a discourtesy to everyone and shows a lack of professionalism. Speaking faster means that your audience will not be able to follow and may stop listening. If you have too much material for the time *cut* or *condense*.

You may wish to write the timings on your cards or on your slide notes, so that when you are delivering your talk you will know how much time you have left at any given moment. This is particularly important with longer speeches or on the occasions when you have to deal with unexpected questions that use up the allocated time.

See your talk as an outline

As a final confidence booster, try giving your talk without using any prompts on your cards. Put your visuals or cards at the other end of the room and attempt a run-through without them. If there are one or two stumbling blocks where you have to refer to them, do so, but continue again without them. This will give you the opportunity to see the talk as an outline or as a series of ideas. If you can visualise the shape, it's often more helpful than trying to remember all the detail. After all, it's probable that you know it, so it's the sequence of points or the logical structure that you need to have at your fingertips.

Dress rehearsals

Dress rehearsals take place at the site and with the visual aids that you intend using. Most of what I want to say about this type of rehearsal is included in Chapter 17, but let me give you one or two suggestions about 'dress'.

Try practising at home in front of the mirror or on video dressed in the clothes that you will be wearing for your presentation or talk. This helps your body language to look natural. I have seen men and women casually try to put their hand in a pocket only to discover that their trousers or skirt are too tight and a relaxed gesture turns into a nervous struggle. Wearing the same clothes enables you to practise all your gestures and identify some of those you may want to eliminate. I have a silk scarf which I love wearing, but because it keeps slipping, I tend to retie it repeatedly. Fortunately a co-trainer told me how distracting he found this, particularly when I was giving a lecture on distracting mannerisms! Now I only wear that scarf with a brooch securely pinning it so that it cannot move.

Watch out for fingers fiddling with rings, cuff links or watches, or constantly fastening or unfastening jacket buttons. Some men empty their pockets of everything in order to avoid fiddling, and this also helps to ensure that their jacket sits smoothly. Wear the same shoes to practise in that you will for your talk. Are they comfortable, or are you likely to move from foot to foot because your shoes are pinching? Naturally you will make sure that your trousers have a sharp crease and your shoes are well polished. A speaker who stands in front of an audience in a badly ironed shirt, creased trousers and a jacket bulging over a large stomach does not help his presentation. A woman with a skirt that's a size too small, hair falling into her eyes and too much jewellery doesn't help her case either.

SUMMARY

- Ensure that you allow enough time to practise several times.

- Use gestures and vary your voice.

- Try using a tape recorder and/or video camera.

- Practise in front of friends and colleagues and ask for feedback.

- You are the most important visual aid to your talk. Make sure that even before you open your mouth the audience feels that you are an enthusiastic and interesting speaker.

PART THREE

Practicalities

16

Writing and Reading
Scripts for Conferences

'Some passages write themselves – others become
a forest of barbed wire and balloons.'
RT HON ENOCH POWELL, MP

Earlier in this book I suggest that using notes is more effective
than reading from a script. However, there may be occasions
when a script is essential, for instance during large audio-visual
conferences. You may choose to read from a paper script or
from autocue; whichever method you use, your first step is to
come up with a good script. In this chapter I show you how to
write and read a script. Also provided is a useful checklist for
speaking at conferences.

How to Write Spoken English

As I have been writing this book I have been imagining you
reading it – in fact, I am trying to imagine that I am holding
a conversation with you. It may be a one-sided conversation
but I wanted to 'talk' to you, as I find it easier to talk than
to write. You will have noticed that my style is informal, even

chatty. At first I found it quite difficult to write like this, as I was inhibited by actually having to type the words.

Unless you are a professional scriptwriter or playwright, it's probable that whenever you write, your words will be read and not listened to. Written English is what we are trained to write and you may find it difficult to adopt a different style when you have to write spoken English. If you have ever seen the transcript of someone talking naturally, you'll have noticed that the sentences are short and sometimes even unfinished; the vocabulary may appear repetitious while other words may be rarely used. You'll also see that many of the sentences are ungrammatical, although the speaker may be well educated. If you write a script that is grammatically correct, it may sound rather formal. For example, in answer to 'Who is it?' how many people say 'It is I'? Most will say 'It's me.' It may be grammatically correct to say 'For whom is that telephone call?' but most people will say 'Who's that phone call for?'

Use *simple vocabulary*. It's not only grammar that changes when we write to speak; it's also the choice of words and the style of sentence. Undoubtedly, your written vocabulary is larger than your spoken vocabulary. However, if you employ words that are not in everyday use, although they may look right on paper, they will sound artificial when spoken. You are not seeking to impress your audience with your academic knowledge – your objective should be to explain your ideas clearly and precisely, so that your audience understands immediately. Of course, if you normally use an extensive vocabulary in your everyday speech and you're sure that your audience will understand, you shouldn't feel inhibited in using it. If you have difficulty in pronouncing a word, don't use it, because under stress you'll stumble and appear uncomfortable.

Here is an example of written vocabulary: 'Successful scriptwriters should ensure that they utilise a vocabulary that is comprehensible to a specific audience.' Translated into spoken English, this becomes: 'Make sure you only use words your audience understands.'

Short, simple sentences are best

Sentence structure can cause problems for novice scriptwriters as they tend to use too many conjunctions (like, and, so, however, but, nevertheless, and so on) and not enough full stops. A useful exercise when you have finished writing your script is to go through it and cross out all conjunctions, and replace them with full stops. It may *look* wrong, but it will *sound* right. The best test of your script is to read it aloud. How does it sound? Would you really express yourself that way? Is it wordy and contrived? It should be natural and simple.

Always ensure that the main point comes at the beginning of your sentence, followed by any qualifying phrases. This is the exact reverse of correct written English. Here is an example of correct written English: 'Provided that our new warehouse is open in July and our sales for domestic appliances continue to grow in Germany, I am going to recommend that we expand our export drive to France.' Here is the same sentence translated into spoken English: 'I am going to recommend we expand our export drive to France. Of course that's provided that our new warehouse is open in July and our sales for domestic appliances continue to grow in Germany.' This sequence of ideas is important because as listeners we cannot hold qualifying phrases in suspension, waiting to hear the total sentence before we can understand the point. You may know what the end of your sentence is, but your listeners won't.

More pitfalls to avoid

When we compose written English, we often use the passive voice, for example, 'Hand movements are to be controlled by speakers when addressing an audience.' If you write like this in your script, it will sound academic and remote. Instead, use an active voice, for example, 'You should control your hand movements when you're addressing an audience.'

Remember that when we speak, we abbreviate words. Cannot becomes can't, would not becomes wouldn't. Make sure your script does not have any unabbreviated words or you will read them out and it will sound artificial. Have you ever heard speakers refer to the 'point above'? In spoken English this should be 'my last point' or 'the point I've just made'.

How to Type a Script

Here are some suggestions on the layout of your script that will make it easier to read. Remember that the lighting at the lectern may not be very bright and therefore your script must be clear and well spaced.

- Use a large typeface and use both upper and lower case for clarity.

- Use double or triple spaces between lines and twice that between paragraphs.

- Use wide margins so that your eyes have less distance to travel along each line.

- Only type on one side of the paper to avoid confusion.

- Spell out numbers in words, for example, three thousand four hundred and fifty pounds and not £3,450 as it's easier to read.

- Avoid continuing a sentence from one page to another.

- Number each page.

- It's unnecessary to staple pages together.

- In the margin mark in colour the point when visual aids should be shown or changed.

Hints on Reading a Script

I have already described the disadvantages of reading a script, but there may be occasions when you can't avoid it. You may want to ensure that no essential points are omitted that could lead to misunderstanding, particularly if you are likely to be quoted by the press or when your words may be legally binding; you could be presenting a particularly sensitive policy statement or you may be making a speech for a political party.

Reading a paper

For some reason there is a tradition that scientific or technical papers are read. I find this discourteous to the audience as they have come to hear a talk and not a 'reading'. If you are presenting a paper at a conference or convention, you may also have to submit your speech in advance so that it can be given to the delegates in the conference folder. If this is the case, consider how you can enliven your presentation with additional new material – do you have any anecdotes or personal stories that might illustrate the main points of your talk? These might be unsuitable for inclusion in the paper that is distributed to the conference delegates, but they would add to the audience's enjoyment of your talk. You could explain some of the problems you have encountered and any doubts that you may have had about resolving them. In this way, the audience will gain from having come to listen to you; if you simply read a script to them with no personal additions, they might feel that they could have stayed at home and read it for themselves. Pay them the compliment of disclosing more of yourself than you might want to put into the paper.

Complex Audio-visual Productions

You will need to have a written script if you are reading your talk from a teleprompter. If you are involved in an elaborate production with slide presentations, video and technical support, you may be expected to give voice cues to the technician. He will be following your script and, as you reach certain words, he will activate the appropriate visual. It is possible to work without a script on this kind of production, but it can lead to mistakes such as the wrong visual appearing or visuals getting out of synchronisation. This looks unprofessional and loses credibility for the speaker.

Using a Teleprompter

A few years ago only TV presenters used teleprompters – often also called autocue (which is, in fact, a brand name). Then it was discovered by politicians and now it's not uncommon to find it in front of speakers at conferences and international seminars.

It consists of a transparent screen placed in front of you and on to which your script is projected. The audience can see your face through the screen and, as you read the words on the screen, you appear to be looking through it at the audience. Your script is relayed by closed-circuit TV cameras through monitors near to the speaking point. From the monitor it's reflected on to the screen in front of you. The operator, off-stage and hidden from the audience, carefully follows the speed at which you are speaking and moves the script as you read it.

Advantages of using a teleprompter

When using a teleprompter you can read your entire script and seem to maintain eye contact with the audience. With several display screens in appropriate positions, you can walk about and appear to be talking naturally with no notes or prompts. Even sophisticated audiences who recognise the display screens will quickly forget that they are being used once the speaker starts to talk.

If you use spectacles to read, you may find that you don't need them to read a teleprompter as the print is very large with only four words to the line. This is particularly helpful if you normally have the problem of having to take off your spectacles in order to look at the audience or at your notes.

How to use a teleprompter like a pro

Make sure your script is sent to the teleprompt company with enough time to make last-minute changes; when several speakers want to modify and amend their talks at the eleventh hour, there could be problems for the audio-visual production team. Remember that they operate from voice cues, so if you change your script you must reposition the cues to indicate when your visuals should be projected. Send your script approximately five to seven days before the date of your presentation so that it can be typed out for the teleprompt camera.

Avoid adding too many instructions to yourself, such as 'Chairman crosses over to left of stage. I introduce guest speaker.' TV scripts are full of stage instructions and the professional overlooks them, but you will only find them confusing if you see them on the screen. The teleprompt display screen is approximately 300mm by 200mm and shows six to seven lines, so if you fill the screen with instructions, you will need to pause for a few moments before you continue speaking.

Ask for a copy of your script as it will appear, so that you can practise reading it aloud. It's useful to become familiar with the four words per line format.

Allow at least two full run-throughs with the teleprompt

company at the venue of your conference or meeting. Often you will find that coaching in the use of this type of teleprompter is included in the hire charge.

The height of the screen can be adjusted for different speakers; however, if the screen is placed vertically, this allows for a greater range of speakers' heights without the need for adjustment.

Use at least two screens at each lectern to give you the flexibility to move your head more naturally from side to side.

Some teleprompter don'ts

• Don't stare at the screen – look away from time to time.

• Don't speak too quickly – the operator will move the script according to the speed of your delivery.

• Don't clutch the lectern – make appropriate hand gestures.

• Don't keep your head in a rigid position – relax and move it naturally.

• Don't frown – look pleasant and remember to smile!

How to make your script sound natural

I have suggested techniques you can follow to write a script in spoken English and not written English, but words alone will not convince your audience. Most of your impact must come from your voice and your visual appearance. Reading a script limits your body language, so you must rely on your voice to express enthusiasm and vitality. Few people are naturally good readers, but it is a skill you can learn through practice.

How a teleprompter works

Final warning

If you have a good, natural script and you learn to use the teleprompter well, it can help you to be a better speaker, but you must allow sufficient time to become familiar with the technique. You have to learn to *read well*; but recognise that not everyone can do this and you may find that you feel more confident using another form of delivery.

Reading Aloud

If you have small children use them as an excuse to read aloud; they are an uncritical audience and will enjoy hearing the full range of your voice. This is an opportunity for you to experiment with exaggeration – loud and soft, fast and slow, high and low. Use the full repertoire of your vocal range.

If you do not have children you can still read aloud from a newspaper, book or play. Learn to read ahead a few words, look up at an imaginary audience and deliver those words. With practice you will feel less dependent on the text. The more eye contact you can make with the audience, the more they will listen.

Practise, practise, practise

Once you have the typed copy of your script, read it aloud straight through. You will find that there are many words that sound *awkward* and sentences that feel *clumsy*. Amend them so that they sound and feel comfortable for you. If you have the misfortune to have to read a script prepared by someone else you will need to allow extra time to personalise it. Don't feel that the scriptwriter is the expert and that the words are cast in stone. I have seen too many speakers stumbling their way through unfamiliar words and sentence constructions, embarrassing both the audience and themselves in the process. You must be the judge of what sounds natural for you, so modify, cut and add until you feel at ease with the script. Do, however, put a time limit on making the changes or you will only have a final draft minutes before you are due to speak!

I was called to train a senior manager two days before an annual conference at which she was due to speak and although the script had been prepared for her, she had failed to find time to read it before our first training session. We spent several hours together, as I encouraged her to read and reread the entire talk out loud. Eventually she was able to inject some colour into her voice as well as make eye contact with the audience.

You don't need a speech consultant to sit with you. Save yourself money and use your own self-discipline to rehearse several times. But silent readings don't count; you must do it out loud.

Try these techniques

Practise reading ahead and raising your eyes as you say the last few words of each sentence. Look down, read the first few words of the next sentence, look up, and deliver them to your audience.

- Slow down and don't gabble because you have the full text in front of you – remember how effective pauses can be.

- Use your full voice repertoire – vary the speed and the pitch, use loud and soft for emphasis.

- Try to keep your head up so that your voice carries further.

- Use facial expression to add impact to your talk.

- You don't need to turn over each page as you finish the last line; simply slide it across face upwards.

- If you need spectacles don't keep removing them during your speech. Use half-glasses and look over the top of them, simply letting your eyes come up and sweep over the rows of faces. Alternatively, you could try using contact lenses, bi-focals or varifocals.

- Remember to arrange for a lectern on which you can rest your speech.

- Practise with a tape recorder or a video camera until you sound and look as if you are talking naturally.

Establishing Contact Before You Begin to Read

Reading a script may make you seem impersonal and remote, but you can reduce this effect by establishing contact with your audience before you begin reading. Start with a personal story you can deliver without referring to your script or involve the audience by asking them a question. 'How many of you came here by public transport? Please raise your hand if you did.'

I once began a talk on controlling nerves by walking to the front of the stage and asking how many people would feel nervous in my position. Up shot the hands. Then I asked one or two of them to describe how they felt when they were nervous. Then I involved other people in the audience by asking whether they shared these symptoms. This short involving technique immediately raised the audience's interest level. Use a similar technique before you begin to read a script, and you will reveal more of yourself than you can when you are hidden behind a lectern.

Reading is a poor method of communicating your thoughts, but at least if you have a good script and can deliver it well, you have a better chance of keeping your listeners' attention. Finally, do remember what one wit said: 'Reading a script is like courting through a fence – you can hear every word but there's not a lot of contact.'

Checklist for Conference Appearances

- *Introduction*   Make sure that the chairperson has a couple of paragraphs about you so that he can introduce you appropriately.

- *Delegates' pack*   If your paper or presentation is to be given to the delegates, make sure that the actual talk you give has additional or different examples and anecdotes to bring it alive. You don't want the whole audience reading your script along with you.

- *Timing*   Always aim to speak for less time than your time slot; for a twenty-minute slot aim for fifteen minutes. Most speakers overrun in the heat of the moment and the conference organisers will be delighted if you underrun.

- *Other speakers* Contact them in advance so that you don't overlap in your subject material. If you are a woman also check that your clothes won't colour clash. (It is advisable to find out the background colour of the stage setting for the same reason. Your favourite blue outfit might make you practically invisible against a stage backdrop of the same colour.)

- *Microphones* Find out what is being provided. Are they fixed on the lectern, or are they radio mikes with power packs? Always ask for the latter so that you can move around on the platform.

- *Visual aids* How will the visuals be projected? Who has control of them? Are they operated by the speaker or by a technician?

- *Question time* Find out in advance how questions are going to be handled. Are they through a chairperson or will each speaker select questions from the floor? Will there be questions for individual speakers or a panel discussion at the end of each session?

- *Rehearsal* Check when you have entry to the venue and ensure that you have a complete run-through in situ with your visual aids and using the microphone. Practise crossing the stage if necessary from your seated position to the lectern.

- *Lights* In large conferences you sometimes can't see the audience because of spotlights on your face. You may be able to ask for the house lights to be turned up so the audience is not in total darkness.

- *Audience* Mix with them before the talk if possible. Ask them what they are interested in. Encourage them to ask you questions at the end. If you can identify a few faces when you begin to speak, it will help to calm your nerves.

• *Speaking* It is better to come out from behind the lectern, even if only for a minute or two. In advance check that the audience can see more than the top of your head when you are behind the lectern and if not ask for a step to stand on.

• *Body language* The bigger the audience the bigger the gestures and facial expressions need to be.

• *Voice* Remember that during a slide presentation most of the audience's attention is on the screen so your voice has to be more interesting.

SUMMARY

• When writing your script don't worry excessively about the grammar.

• Use simple but precise words and keep your sentences short.

• Abbreviate words like cannot, do not, should not, and so on to make them sound less stilted.

• Read the script aloud several times to test its naturalness and until it becomes familiar.

• Practise reading aloud from newspapers or from a book.

• Learn to read ahead and look up at the audience.

17

Visiting the Venue

'Stop. Look. Listen.'
RALPH UPTON
(notice devised in 1912 for US railway crossings)

Whether you've planned to talk to a small gathering of your colleagues or a group of friends, or to give a speech to delegates at a major conference, it is important to check out the venue for your presentation. In this chapter I explore some of the essential areas to consider. I have divided up the chapter according to the size of the venue.

Where Are You Speaking?

You will probably be talking in one of the following situations:

- around-the-table, formal and informal meetings, generally with a group of less than twelve, on your own premises or off-site, with work colleagues or people of the same community, for example residents' association meeting, departmental meeting or board meeting;

- social function where people remain standing, for example a cocktail reception, leaving party or networking event;

- meeting with a medium-sized audience of twenty or more, in an off-site venue such as a meeting or conference room in a hotel, for a regional gathering or regular sales management meeting;

- large sit-down lunch or dinner for over a hundred people;

- conference in a meeting room in a hotel or conference centre with large audience of over 150 people.

The Visit

It's always advisable to attempt to visit the site where you will be talking, allowing sufficient time to change or rectify any details that might prevent you from presenting well and efficiently. I know that this is sometimes not possible – if, say, you are in Edinburgh and your client is in Paris – but even if you see the room ten minutes before the meeting is due to start, this will enable you to familiarise yourself with the layout and make minor changes. In the case of larger conferences it is obviously critical that you spend time at the venue before you speak. Listed below are the points that you should bear in mind when you are visiting sites of different sizes.

Small Venues

Checklist for small venues

Although with small groups it is tempting to ignore the need to organise the space, in some ways the environment can have more impact on them than on a larger group.

- Ask yourself how you want the audience sitting. Do they need tables? Would a semi-circle without tables facing the speaker be a better arrangement? Are there any members you want sitting together or separated or close to you? Can everyone see each other, you and the screen (if you are using visual aids)? Do you need to remove spare chairs to create a friendlier and intimate atmosphere?

- Is there adequate space for your notes, visual aids and handouts? Are there cups or paper left over from a previous meeting that would be better removed? Can you escape from the barrier of a table between you and the audience, or will you be trapped behind it? Where will you position your flip chart and projector?

- Where are the sockets for the equipment? Will you need an extension lead?

- How do you dim the lights if you need to? Is a pointer available to you to identify details on the screen? How can you adjust the heating or air conditioning? Can you open the windows?

- Who is providing tea/coffee and at what time? Your entire presentation could be jeopardised by the appearance of refreshments at a critical moment!

- Is there a clock in the room? Or should you take your own? It's often easier to read a small clock than your wristwatch, even if you remove it and place it in front of you.

- Who is providing pens, pads, drinking water?

Dress rehearsal for small groups

You may feel that for a small group presentation a dress rehearsal is not necessary. However, I urge you to stand in the

Theatre style

Classroom style

Classroom style

Seating diagrams

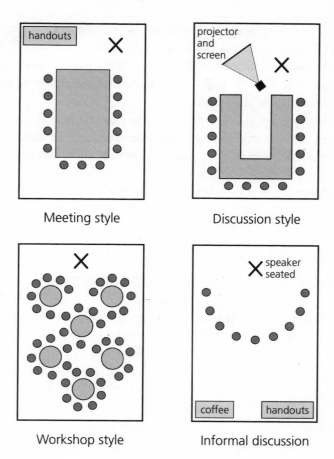

Meeting style

Discussion style

Workshop style

Informal discussion

Seating diagrams

spot where you will be speaking and, at least once, rehearse out loud. This is particularly important if you are using visual aids, as you want to be sure that all the equipment works and that you feel confident using it.

In a small room, you should sit in all the seats to ensure the screen is visible from all positions. If possible, ask someone to take your place as speaker so that you can check you will not be obscuring the screen when you are addressing the group. I often find in such a group that I have to stand to one side when a visual is showing so that I am not in the way (read Chapters 6 and 7 on visual aids for more information on this). While rehearsing, move from the flip chart to the projector and across the area that is your 'stage' and check that no cables or junction boxes are in your path.

While you are rehearsing, remember to retime your talk on site and allow sufficient time for your audience to absorb the information contained in your visual aids. In a small group, there is a greater likelihood of interruptions and questions from your audience during your talk and therefore I suggest you plan to talk for five minutes less than your allocated slot so that you keep within the time limit.

Dress rehearsals for team presentations

If you find it difficult to rehearse by yourself, it will take even greater discipline and courage to insist that those who are jointly presenting with you should rehearse as a team. I know how easy it is to outline roughly what each of you will do and casually reassure each other that it will be fine on the day. This is a big mistake. You should all have a very clear idea exactly what part of the presentation you will be covering, as well as how you will hand over to each other and whether one member can supply additional information if someone else omits it. I have seen terrible glares directed at someone who thought she was being helpful when she chipped in with an important point that the speaker had apparently forgotten. This kind of team support can be invaluable, but be sure to arrange between you how it is to be handled, otherwise it can cause bad feeling. Make sure everyone understands their role and the framework in which they are speaking. This may sound too formal to you, but it can be handled in a manner that appears relaxed and casual, and allows everyone to be sure of what is expected of them.

I remember an unsuccessful presentation I made with

another consultant at the beginning of my career in which he misinterpreted a sign from me and continued talking on all the points I was expecting to cover, thus resulting in a rather unbalanced presentation. We had been reluctant to rehearse together as we were sure we knew our stuff – we did, but we hadn't presented as a team before.

If you are working as part of a team, ensure that you have anticipated questions and planned answers, as well as decided which team member should give them. If you are involved with a sales presentation where your prospective clients are judging your company, a united team will go a long way to convincing them that you represent a reliable and successful company.

Medium-sized Venues

Checklist for medium-sized venues

- Check everything on the list for small venues.

- If you are using a hotel, check the name of the manager in charge of hiring the room you are to use and find out whether she will be on duty on the day of your event.

- What time will you be able to get into the room?

- Are the chairs comfortable? Can they be substituted by better ones if your function is long? Ensure that surplus chairs will be removed. Remember to provide a seating layout plan.

- Make sure that no telephones in the meeting room will ring and disturb you.

- If you are using visual aids ask to see the equipment. Are you familiar with the projector? Do you know how to focus this particular model? What type of screen will be provided? (See Chapters 6 and 7 on visual aids.)

- If you are using a lectern, how high is it? Does it have a light so that you can read your notes if the main lights are dimmed?

- Are you operating your own visual aids and, if not, what cues will you give to the technician?

- Check where the lighting switches are and who will operate them. Can only half the room be dimmed if necessary? Do the windows need to be covered?

- Where are the toilets and the fire escapes?

- What facilities does the hotel offer for taking messages?

- If refreshments are to be served will they be in the meeting room or in an adjacent room? If it is in the same room, ensure that the crockery is laid out before the meeting. You don't want to give your talk to the accompaniment of rattling china.

- If you are speaking after a formal meal or at a place where drinks and canapés are served ensure that the waiting staff have been instructed to refrain from serving or clearing up while you are presenting.

Dress rehearsal for medium-sized groups

As the visual back-up becomes more elaborate and includes additional people, your technical dress rehearsal is even more important. You may not be in direct control of the visuals or lights and the technician will be relying on you for cues. Your dress rehearsal should start at the point where you are first visible to the audience. Rehearse your entrance, including stepping on to the platform. I remember seeing a woman in a tight skirt struggling to get on to the stage. This didn't make a good first impression. Some forethought could have prevented that.

When you are introduced, walk purposefully to your speaking spot, pause, look at the audience, make eye contact and give them your 'I am happy' expression, take a good breath and then start to speak. That silence may feel long to you, but it allows the audience to focus on you and begin to listen. It shows them that you are in control. Novice speakers often start to speak too quickly and deliver in a high and rapid voice that lacks credibility and loses the audience's attention immediately.

Large Venues

For large events, most of the details should be organised by the conference or event coordinator. If that happens to be you, you will need to buy another book, because this is not the place to list everything you need to know. As a speaker your responsibility is to consider every aspect of your own talk and how you can ensure that your presentation will be professional and trouble free. Here are some points to consider:

Checklist for large venues

- Will you speak from your table if it is a dinner/lunch speech or from a platform?
- How will you approach the platform/stage?
- Where will you stand?
- Will there be other people on the stage with you?
- Will you need a teleprompt?
- Can you see the audience or are the lights shining into your eyes?
- If you are using visuals how will they be cued up?

> - What type of microphone is provided? Is it fixed or will you be able to move around?
>
> - Is the text of your talk being distributed to delegates, and if so will it be before or after your presentation?

Dress rehearsal for large groups

One of the most difficult performances I have ever given was in a large conference centre where half a dozen people were scattered about talking to one another and paying no attention to me. Occasionally doors opened and new people came in or shouted out obscure messages. Lights dimmed or suddenly brightened for no apparent reason, and visuals flashed on and off the screen. Through all this, I gave my presentation. Well, if you haven't guessed it already, I was at a dress rehearsal.

Very often they are disorganised but you should make the most of them because every moment of practice will help you to give a professional performance. Take the opportunity of practising your entrance as well as your introduction and your entire talk complete with cued visuals. If you are using a teleprompter for the first time, you will need some additional tuition. It is a knack to be able to use it well, but in order to be effective, you must practise several times. Don't rely on one dress rehearsal to get it right (see Chapter 16 on writing and reading scripts).

Familiarity Breeds Confidence

These are probably the most important three words in this book and if you only follow this advice, you will become a better speaker.

Most of our worries about speaking in public are based on

the fear that we will make fools of ourselves, or worries about what people will think of us. We want the audience to respond and react and our biggest fear is that they won't. In fact it is unlikely that the audience will fail to respond, but in order to realise this, we need confidence.

Unfortunately you can't conjure confidence out of the air; it will only come with practice. Your audience will believe in you if you believe in yourself. Practising gives you confidence and enthusiasm – a winning formula.

SUMMARY

- Find out as early as possible where you will be doing your presentation.

- Always visit the venue to make sure everything you need is there.

- For large meetings, conferences and important social events, try to book time for a rehearsal at the site before the big day.

- Remember that knowing about the site and its facilities will help you feel more confident.

18

Interacting with Your Audience

'Pretend everyone has a sign on their chest which reads –
"Make me feel important."'

TERRY PAULSON, American motivational speaker

I've said earlier that I regard anyone who is listening to you to be your audience, but obviously a large group behaves differently from an informal gathering of five or six people. So how you interact will depend on the size of the group you will be addressing.

We know that no one listens with total concentration and anyone can be distracted by you, the speaker, as well as by their own internal thoughts. Now you need to consider the dynamics of the group and the interaction between the different members. I have divided up this section according to the size of the audience, whether they are small, medium or large.

Speaking to Small Groups

The interaction within a small group is often visible. Also be aware that each person may be interpreting your message at two levels – their own, and how they imagine others are receiving it. Other people influence how we react to things. For instance, watching a sexy film on TV with a close friend may be fun but becomes a totally different experience if an elderly relative is also in the room. You have probably been in the situation where you have a good working relationship with one or two people and find that they act differently when joined by others. Sometimes they are reluctant to express their views or opinions in a group and may need encouragement from you.

You should bear in mind the personalities and relationships that exist within a group when you are presenting your ideas. Remember to maintain eye contact with everyone; it can be tempting to only look at a friendly face or at the most senior member whom you wish to impress and avoid looking at someone who you feel may disagree with you.

Discover personal barriers and relationships

Within your own organisation or group you will be aware of conflicts or liaisons that exist between people. Meetings with other people, where you are not so familiar with the internal politics, can be more difficult. Use any contacts you already have to learn about your audience. It can be helpful to know of any quirks and personal likes and dislikes. For instance, the style of dress which is considered appropriate for a meeting depends on the culture of an organisation. One of my clients, a creative and artistic film director, failed to obtain financial backing for a project because of his colourful shirt and casual jacket. His bank manager didn't think he was serious enough to justify a loan. However, I have heard the story that Lord King, when he was chairman of British Airways, said of Richard Branson of Virgin, 'If he'd worn a suit, we would have taken him more seriously.' So it can work in your favour.

Find out as much as you can about the listeners so that your message will be accepted and not rejected by their own personal barriers. Speaking to an unknown audience can be like crossing a minefield, but if you do your research you should be able to get through and achieve your goals.

It may be impossible to find out anything in depth before meeting your listeners so set aside the first few minutes of your presentation to ask them questions. This is an opportunity to practise your listening skills, and their answers will help you tailor your material to their needs. You don't need to change the core of your talk, but you can use the audience's experiences as examples. By doing this your ideas will be personalised for them and are more likely to be accepted. This interaction is a luxury that you don't have when speaking to larger groups so take advantage of it.

At Speak First we always allow time for the participants to introduce themselves at the beginning of the course; this allows the trainer to tailor the course to each participant's needs. On one occasion I remember a student telling me early on in the day that her talks had been criticised for lacking structure, so when we reached that stage in the training course I was able to point out to her how she could plan her future talks for greater clarity.

Find out who will be there: their position and power; their relationship with each other; their attitude to you or your organisation or products/services; and any previous knowledge and experience of the subject of your talk.

Interpreting the body language of your audience and responding to it

In Chapter 11 on looking confident I emphasised the importance of eye contact, because an audience will stop listening if they feel you are not interested in them – looking at them shows that you are.

Watching the faces of your audience has another important advantage – it enables you to see how they are receiving what you are saying. In a small group this is particularly important because you can react to them. If someone is looking puzzled, you can check that they have understood: 'Ian, would you like me to expand on that point?' Someone may nod in agreement and you can involve them by saying, 'Sue, you look as if you have had some experience of that yourself.'

By placing their name at the beginning of your question, you alert them to the fact that you are talking directly to them and they can either decline or accept your invitation to speak. Be careful not to look surprised or disappointed if they don't respond, but simply continue with your talk. By speaking directly to them, you have involved them and shown your willingness to include them.

When someone is looking bored or uninterested, you can also ask them a question to allow them to express their thoughts, but if they do not answer, try not to be distracted by their lack of interest. I hate to see someone smothering a yawn, although I suppose an open yawn is worse. However, I have learnt to ignore it because although it may indicate boredom, it could also be totally unconnected with my talk – a sleepless night due to a sick child, a late-night party or even a sign to the rest of the audience that the 'yawner' is superior and wants to distance herself from the meeting.

The non-verbal interaction between the members of the audience can also show you how your message is being received. Watch out for eye contact between them, as well as nods of agreement or negative signs like a shake of a head. Facial expression reveals much of what a person is thinking and feeling, but you should also pay attention to their bodies. For instance, in general, sitting forwards indicates more interest than sitting back.

You may feel that delivering a talk is difficult enough without closely watching and interpreting body language. In actual fact, I am sure that you are aware of all these signs already, but you may not have realised how you can use them to become a more effective speaker. Audiences want to feel they are important to the speaker and by acknowledging the signs they are giving you (sometimes unconsciously) you are paying them a compliment. See also Chapter 19 on learning to be persuasive.

Other involving techniques

Presenting to a small group is a challenge because you are addressing individuals and you do need to break up your monologue to include them.

You can interpret their thoughts by watching their body language and also prompt their participation by directing a question to anyone who may have a personal contribution: 'John, I believe you used that caterer for your anniversary party – what did you think of them?' or 'Fiona, what particular problems have you come up against using the old system?' In this way, you not only enliven your talk with real-life examples, but you also give the audience another voice to listen to, which will help to extend their concentration span and allow you to speak for longer.

Remember to build 'comprehension questions' into your talk, so that you can check their understanding. Listen carefully to any comments or questions, but confine your answers to the material you have already presented and don't be tempted to reveal part of the rest of your talk. If you use 'comprehension questions' you will be involving the audience but remaining in control of the situation.

How to cope with interruptions from a small audience

So much for the techniques of involving your audience, but what do you do when the audience involves itself by interrupting? How can you deal with them? Try to remember that you are in charge, that it is your show and that you should control what happens.

Let's imagine that you are in full flow and a member of the audience asks a very relevant question. It is up to you to decide how to handle the situation. If you feel that you can respond and continue with your talk without a falter, do so. However, many speakers are distracted by questions and find it difficult to resume their flow if they stop. If you are one of these, I suggest you lay down some ground rules before you begin speaking. Suggest that you would like to take questions at the end, but if anyone has difficulty following your talk, they should ask you to explain more fully.

The main advantage of keeping in control and not letting people interrupt you is that you stick to your predetermined structure, which you have designed to enable the audience to follow easily a logical sequence of points. Even if *you* have no problem in presenting your material in a haphazard manner in order to answer questions as they occur, your audience will be confused and may find it difficult to follow.

Chapter 14 deals more fully with handling questions, but you also need to be aware at this stage of the reasons why people ask questions.

Often it's because they want more information or don't understand a particular point. They may, however, see it as an opportunity to be controversial or witty in front of their boss or subordinates. If you suspect that this is the case, answer politely but don't allow yourself to be drawn into an argument or a discussion. You can remind the questioner that you have not finished your presentation and that you would like to return to the question at the end.

You may find yourself in a position of being unable to say, 'I'll answer that later.' If your boss or a client asks you a question in the middle of your presentation, you may feel obliged to answer it. Do so using the minimum number of words and say that you find it easier to present the whole talk so that the questioner can see it in its entirety. I have seen a one-hour meeting spread over the whole afternoon because the speaker allowed himself to be interrupted. Remember that the concentration span of your audience is limited and if you don't keep control their minds will wander and your ideas will not be accepted or even remembered.

Speaking to Medium-sized Audiences

You will find that a group of more than twenty people has a different character from a smaller group, as each member loses some individuality and takes on the identity of the group. As a speaker your eye contact is more general and therefore the audience feels less involved; they may feel that there is less need for them to concentrate because they are less visible.

Think of how you feel in a group of five, fifteen, fifty and a hundred and fifty and you will see how an increased number of people changes the quality of the group.

Interaction with the medium-sized audience

I consider a group of twenty to thirty as a medium-sized audience and you'll realise that you can't have the same personal interaction with each member as you can with a smaller group. Although you should be aware of the audience's body language, you can only address that which appears to be most common: it may be possible to ignore one person looking puzzled but half a dozen puzzled faces indicates that further explanations are necessary.

How to control the medium-sized audience

It is more important with a larger group to keep control as there is greater potential for disorganisation if you allow yourself to be side-tracked by spontaneous questions and comments. Do let them know that you want to keep interruptions to the minimum, and provided you smile when you say this, no one will take offence; if you tell them how valuable you know their time to be and that you don't want to waste it, you should find that they will cooperate.

Should you sit or stand?

Always stand if you possibly can. In some organisations there is a tradition that speakers stay sitting and it takes a brave soul to break the convention. Try to be that brave soul. You will feel awkward and self-conscious to start with, but you will look and sound more powerful. Explain that you want to stand so that everyone can see you and so that your voice carries better.

Try not to rest your hands on the table in front of you, but stand tall and confidently project your voice to the furthest person (to overcome the sound of air conditioning, people coughing and shuffling papers, and so on), and maintain eye contact with as many people as possible. Remember to push your chair well back or even stand behind it, and make sure your briefcase or handbag is not in the way of your feet. If possible stand without barriers – table or desk – between you and your audience. Your path to the flip chart or other visual aids should be clear, and if your handouts are to be distributed during the talk, ensure that they are in two or three central locations, so that this can be accomplished quickly and with little disruption.

To give a professional presentation and achieve your objectives you must consider every small detail, because you want the audience's attention focused on your talk and not on some minor distraction. Take a few minutes before you begin to speak to check the area around your feet for any obstacles, and to check the space you have for hand and arm gestures; enthusiastic gestures are very effective provided they don't knock somebody on the head.

Include everyone with eye contact. By varying your gaze, you can avoid the tennis game effect – right, left; right, left.

Speaking to Large Audiences

When you can't see the whites of their eyes, you're addressing a large audience and entering the realm of public speaking. Often individual eye contact is impossible except for those people close to you, but you still need to look in the direction of as many people as possible. If you are part of a panel and sitting on a platform remember to include other speakers and the chairperson. Your body language should be more exaggerated and, in particular, be sure to smile more than if you are speaking to a smaller group – a person at the back of a big room or banqueting hall will be able to discern a proper smile, but will not see a small movement such as a raised eyebrow; a friendly expression is going to be very effective even when talking at a serious business conference.

Researching two hundred people

You need to research a large audience as much as a smaller group. If you are speaking at a social event find out as much as you can from the people who are organising it. If you are speaking within your own company or organisation, you'll have no problem finding out what you need to know. However, if you are addressing a large group who have come independently to a public conference, you will need to address your questions to the organisers. Find out:

• how and why the audience is coming;

• what was written in the announcement of the event or conference;

• who else will be speaking and on what aspect of the topic;

See also Chapter 2 'Hassle-free Preparation and Planning'.

I like to contact the other speakers to check that I will not overlap with their material. Also, if another woman is appearing, I ask what colour she'll be wearing so that my choice of outfit doesn't clash with hers.

It always surprises me to see how speakers fail to chat to their audiences at coffee breaks and meal times. I find these times an invaluable source of material and will often refer to a conversation I have had with a member of the audience before my talk. For example, I say, 'Someone was telling me during the coffee break that ...' and this leads into my next point. It has the advantage of showing the audience that you are approachable and that you can relate to their problems and experiences. You also benefit from speaking face to face with the individuals who are your audience. It is also more relaxing than trying to fit in a final mental rehearsal.

Prepare for interruptions

If you are speaking at a formal conference there will be fewer interruptions. However, you should plan how you would deal with any odd questions that may come in the middle of your speech. At social events like weddings and birthdays you may have to handle friends who, having consumed large quantities of liquid hospitality, want to help you out with your speech.

Using common identity in large audiences

As a general rule it is more difficult to maintain a high degree of attention with a large audience than a small one, because they are likely to be distracted by their own thoughts and you can't use as much personal involvement. Therefore take advantage of the fact that they will act as a group in many instances. Laughter is infectious and an amusing story that might only raise a smile when told to an individual will get a more significant response from a larger audience. Humour is also a great unifier and if you can use it to relax the audience, they will appreciate you as a speaker. In large groups, if you can appeal to their common hopes and fears, their shared experiences, their admiration and contempt, they will respond to you. See also Chapter 13 on using humour.

Understanding their concentration span

Audiences can only concentrate on one speaker for a limited period of time, after which they listen less attentively and eventually become fidgety and bored. The concentration span depends on a number of factors:

- their initial interest in the subject;
- the time of day – people tend to be most attentive first thing in the morning and least attentive after lunch, particularly if they have been drinking alcohol; speakers know this period as the Graveyard Slot;
- whether or not they think the speaker will expect them to answer a question;
- their own opinion and assessment of the speaker;
- their need to know about the subject.

Generally, an audience will concentrate most during the first ten minutes of a talk and their interest will remain on a low plateau until they hear the words, 'Finally, let me conclude by saying ...'

From this you can see that you need to state your main message strongly at the beginning of the talk and repeat it at the end.

Ideally, one speaker should not talk for more than twenty minutes. I know that in many situations this is not practical, so I suggest a maximum of forty minutes. If you need to speak for a longer period, consider splitting the time slot between two speakers. Be sure to work closely with one another, rehearsing together, and remember to plan ahead of time how you will deal with questions, so that you can give a united performance.

How to use interest prompts

There is frequently a low period in the middle of the concentration span and it's up to you to include interest prompts in your talk to keep the audience's attention. Here are some which you might find useful.

Change your position

If you are using a lectern come out from behind it and move to centre stage; in a smaller room, move from a flip chart to stand closer to one of the listeners. If you have been sitting, stand, and vice versa. In an informal setting, consider perching on the edge of a table in order to vary your position.

Use a visual aid

Be careful not to use a visual aid only as an interest prompt (see Chapters 6 and 7 on visual aids). Write on the flip chart, show a slide or pass round a sample. I saw a very effective use of props at a farewell party for a retiring director who had collected together items of interest spanning several years which he handed round during his speech.

Ask a question

Involve the audience by asking one of the following kinds of questions:

1. Rhetorical – the listeners will be prompted to give a mental response. Example: 'Where will we all be this time next year?'

2. General question answered by a show of hands. Example: 'Who has installed a new computer system in the last year? Put up your hand.'

3. General question answered by one or two people with a direct answer. Example: 'Who here can give me the details of a problem that they have encountered getting through to the Help Desk?'

4. Direct question. Example: 'Mr Smith, what did you do when the fire destroyed all your records?'

Except for 1 above, always wait for an answer; the audience needs time to adjust from passive listening to active participation, so don't be afraid of the silence.

Involve the audience in action

• Ask them to work out a calculation, using their own situation as a base and applying the theory which you have just presented.

• Ask the small/medium audience to move to a demonstration table to see a model in action and, better still, get involved in some way.

• Ask for a volunteer to write on the flip chart.

• Ask them to turn to the person sitting next to them and discuss a point raised in your talk.

• Ask them to raise their glasses in a toast.

You'll see in Chapter 2 on preparation and planning that your talk should include several interest prompts at various points to add variety.

Other ways of preventing boredom

During the coffee breaks, if possible open all windows to get a change of air. You could also ask people to stand and stretch.

I once had to speak in the Graveyard Slot, i.e. after lunch, at a conference in a hotel venue, with no windows and to an audience of approximately a hundred business people who had been sitting all the morning and had indulged in a good lunch. What a challenge! As I was addressing them on the importance of presentation skills, I decided to emphasise breathing and voice projection, and asked them to join me in several exercises. After a reluctant start, they all participated and no one had the opportunity of going to sleep.

I have seen the last speaker in a long evening's presentation ask the audience to stand and move about on the spot to get rid of 'dead bums' before she began her talk.

Formal business presentations with senior executives may not be the place to practise some of these techniques, but do be aware that as the speaker you are in control of the audience. If their concentration is lagging, your objectives will not be achieved and your talk will not be remembered.

SUMMARY

- Bear in mind that different-sized audiences behave differently.

- Get to know your audience.

- Keep an eye on their body language and react to it if appropriate.

- Use comprehension questions in small groups.

- Control the interruptions and if necessary refrain from answering questions.

- Use interest prompts to stimulate the audience and retain their attention.

19

Learning to be Persuasive

'You can't learn anything while you are talking.'
BING CROSBY (in BBC interview with Michael Parkinson, 1975)

Interaction with the audience is a universally acceptable goal, but a good speaker is also a good seller. There are some people who think selling is a dirty word. For them, the very idea of a salesperson conjures up a picture of a pushy, fast-talking individual whose sole aim is to force his customers to buy against their will. Worst of all, he doesn't listen. Faced with such a hard sell, his customers may feel that their only option is to sign on the dotted line. Most of us have experienced such horrors at one time or another and they tend to colour our view of selling.

In this chapter I suggest some ways in which you can improve *your* selling techniques because, whether you recognise it or not, you're involved in selling every day of your life. You may wonder how I can make such a claim. Think back over the last few days to the decisions you have made in your working or social environment. Were all your ideas and views totally supported by everyone who was involved? I doubt it. I imagine that you had to coax, influence, cajole, urge, even insist and impel people to follow what you believed to be the right course of action, even if it were only to get your children to go to bed or persuade your partner that football was the best option on TV that evening. In that process you were selling your ideas and your opinions. I have linked persuading, convincing and selling together in one chapter because I believe they are all part of the same skill.

One reason why you may dislike the idea of selling is because, like telling a joke, it requires a positive reaction from the listener, and if the response is not forthcoming, you feel you are being rejected. This is in fact a misconception. It is your opinion or idea that is being rejected, not you. This is a hard lesson to learn. In my early days of selling, I often felt discouraged by a seemingly endless wall of 'No, thank you, dear, not today.' Fortunately I was able to improve my techniques, so eventually I received more acceptances than rejections. In the commercial world the reason for your speaking will often be to persuade, convince and sell. Here I draw together some of the themes that run through this book and show how you can use them to achieve support and agreement for your views more easily.

Prepare to Persuade

Your first step to successful persuasion is researching your listeners. What are their concerns and what are their problems? What do you know about them? It is impossible to persuade them if you don't know their present position. In an extreme case you might find that they already agree with you and need no convincing. Your listeners have views and opinions as well as difficulties and anxieties that will influence their acceptance or rejection of your ideas.

In the next chapter (see page 278) I refer to open questions that managers employ to gain full and comprehensive answers. Open questions generally start with who, what, when, why, where or how. Use them to discover more about your listeners' opinions. 'What do you think the effect will be if we agree to the overtime ban?' 'Who do you support as the members' representative on the committee?' Reverse roles with your listener and let him state his case as fully as possible, but remember also to ask for reasons why he supports a particular view. If you are managing a sales force, you may need to persuade your reps of the importance of completing paperwork. If you can discover their reason for disliking it, you will be halfway to overcoming their prejudice. Sometimes people are reluctant to express their doubts or fears about a course of action because they feel that it will reflect on their ability to complete a task. I am often faced with delegates on a training course who dislike admitting that they feel nervous when speaking in public. I try to persuade them that recognising their anxiety is the first step to handling it.

You may be attempting to convince a friend to change her mind, but until you can uncover the reasons for her views, you won't be successful. Her views may be based on faulty information. 'I don't like Italian restaurants: all the waiters are always too familiar.' She may have had previous experience, which she has misinterpreted or which has jaundiced her thinking. If you don't identify her viewpoint and the reasons for it, your sound and well-reasoned arguments will go sailing straight past her, because they are not correctly targeted. You must have the bull's eye in your sights before you can hit it.

Developing Your Listening Skills

You may need to improve your listening skills before you can persuade successfully. In Chapter 1 (see page 3) I provided reasons why listening isn't easy and suggested some ways in which speakers could help to minimise the difficulties.

You can also help yourself to be a better listener. Remember that some of the major barriers to effective listening are internal. When, as a listener, you go down Route 350, you are allowing yourself to be distracted by your own thoughts. So concentrate and don't allow your own experience and prejudices to block out what you're hearing. Listen with an open mind to the content and disregard the distractions of irritating mannerisms and poor delivery. I find this a great challenge. Much of my working day is spent assessing and correcting speakers, so that it has become second nature. When I am 'off duty' and in a social situation, I have to silence my inner thoughts such as, 'What a pity she doesn't open her mouth more when she speaks' or 'Why does he keep saying yes at the end of every sentence?' Don't fall into the trap of letting poor presentation prevent you from listening well.

Instead of going down Route 350, you can use your spare brain capacity to summarise mentally and to recap on what the speaker is telling you. This can be particularly useful if the speaker is presenting information in a jumbled and unstructured manner. As each idea is presented, you can mentally categorise it so that you'll be able to recall it at a later stage.

Don't forget your body language when you are listening. Your eye contact and facial expression should be encouraging. Show your interest by smiling, nodding, saying, 'I see, I understand,' and asking questions, for example 'So why was that?' Listening needs to be visual to the speaker.

Successful persuasion often depends upon your demonstrating an understanding of the listeners' viewpoint. Showing that you recognise their problem can help to build a rapport that increases your credibility. Don't be too quick to present your own ideas. Register that you have heard what they've told you by repeating their views. This is an indication that you have listened, not that you agree with them. 'So you're worried that if we extend the period of payment, the club members will take advantage?' 'So from your point of view, asking the secretaries to work overtime could lead to resentment?' 'I see, so you're telling me that if you installed new equipment as planned it could cause disruption at a very busy time of year?'

What Are the Needs of Your Listeners?

In Chapter 2 (see page 14), I mentioned satisfying some of the needs of senior management as well as those of the staff. Everyone has their own particular need that they seek to satisfy, as well as problems they want to solve. So find out what your listeners want. Do they have a difficulty that needs resolving? What are they hoping to achieve? What are they aiming for? It may be as simple as an afternoon in which the telephone doesn't ring or as ambitious as doubling the previous year's profits.

I remember a management consultant telling me that when she talked to a new client, she always tried to identify 'the pain'. In other words, what was causing her client anxiety? Her client might identify 'the pain' like this: 'If only we could find staff who took an interest in their jobs . . .' or 'If only we could be sure of getting the spare parts on time . . .' Find out what is your listeners' 'if only'. What is their fantasy? Ask questions and listen to the answers.

Don't Interrupt

With inarticulate, long-winded speakers, it is very tempting to supply words that they are searching for or even to finish their sentences for them. Resist the temptation. It will be seen as an interruption. Don't jump in immediately the speaker has finished speaking, but allow a few seconds' silence. He will know from this that you have been listening and not simply waiting for your turn to speak. Most importantly, he will be ready to listen to you. He will feel that he doesn't have to battle with you for a chance to be heard. Therefore, your chances of persuading him are increased.

What Do They Know and What Do They Think of You?

Now that you understand your listeners' position, you need to discover how much they already know about your views. You may recall from Chapter 2 that this level of knowledge can be multi-layered:

- What do they know?

- What do they think they know?

- What do they want to know?

- What do they need to know in order for you to convince and persuade them?

If your listeners have no background information and you intend to persuade them on a new course of action, you'll need to lay some foundations before you start. But, you'll quickly lose their attention if they feel that you are talking down to them. Don't underestimate the risks of miscalculating your listeners' level of understanding and knowledge.

Don't bore your colleagues in a meeting with historical facts that everyone knows. Don't do the reverse and assume that they already have enough information to understand your presentation. I remember vividly presenting a complex training programme to a board of directors, having already sent a written proposal to the training director. It was only later that I realised the rest of the board had not seen the written proposal and therefore were unable to follow or understand most of my presentation.

You will also need to know what their attitude is towards you and your views. Are they in favour? Are they indifferent? Are they opposed? A listener who is well informed but who is opposed to you will require a different approach from one who is indifferent and uninformed.

More questions and more listening will supply the answers

to help you plan your strategy for successful persuasion. To convince people, you need to appeal to their minds and to their emotions – one supports the other.

Information for Their Minds

Early on in your persuasion, establish why your audience should listen to you. Tell them what's in it for them. For example, 'By following my suggestions I believe that we will get more people to enrol for our social events' or 'I am going to show you various techniques you can use to overcome the backlog in the warehouse.' Remember, you shouldn't tell them that you are going to convince or persuade them that one or other of the techniques is superior. This is, of course, what you may hope to do during your presentation, but it must appear that the decision is left to your listeners.

Expand on what they already know and add new points. If their level of knowledge is minimal, you may decide to present your information in a series of talks, rather than at one session. There is a limit to the amount of new material that can be absorbed at any one time. As you present the reasons for your opinions, remember to identify the areas of mutual agreement: 'You will see that we both agree on . . .' In this manner you will demonstrate your acceptance of some of your listeners' views that will provide a favourable climate in which to discuss the more controversial points. Try to minimise your differences and discount your minor points of disagreement, so that you can concentrate on persuading them to accept your views on the larger issues.

Remember that you need to summarise constantly and to recap. Make sure that your persuasive talk also has an easy-to-follow structure and that your ideas are illustrated with relevant examples.

Persuasion at Meetings

Various estimates have been made about the total number of hours people spend in meetings every year and assessments have also been made on the total cost of these meetings. In your next idle moment, maybe at an unproductive meeting, look around the room and calculate how much time is being spent in having the people involved sitting at the table. In the business world, you can see how companies benefit financially by reducing the amount of time mangers spend at inefficient meetings.

How to lead a discussion

Many of the skills you will need for leading a discussion have already been referred to in earlier chapters. Your planning and preparation for a meeting should fall under the same three headings:

- setting an objective;

- researching your audience;

- designing a structure.

Setting an objective

Many meetings are held for the wrong reasons. Groups may follow traditional patterns of behaviour – 'We always have a meeting on Thursdays' – and it is often necessary to question the real purpose. Some of the more common reasons are:

- solving problems;

- giving and getting information;

- taking decisions;

- presenting and selling ideas and concepts.

If you are responsible for the meeting you must be clear why it is taking place and what you hope it will achieve. Make sure that a memo or a couple of phone calls couldn't accomplish as much, but in less time.

Researching your audience

All the questions you asked in preparation for being persuasive are relevant here. You should try and limit the number of people attending. An ideal number is between six and seven; when there are more than ten present, meetings become unmanageable. Divide up larger groups so that your discussion is more productive. Make sure everyone is aware of the purpose and of their role in the meeting. Don't invite anyone who is not essential for achieving your objective. 'Assistants' who accompany their bosses are usually superfluous – you probably need one or the other but not both.

Designing a structure

Your preparation must include a detailed agenda that is circulated well in advance so that everyone has a chance to prepare. Decide whether to schedule items in order of importance or of length. Beware of short, unimportant items, like deciding the new position of the noticeboard, which can develop into a half-hour discussion. You can often assess the likely time needed for a particular item by talking to the people concerned. If they appear to be in total disagreement you may decide to have a pre-meeting to sort out some of their differences. This will make more efficient use of the time scheduled for the main discussion.

The structure of a problem-solving discussion could be designed like this:

• describe the problem;

• discuss the background and the reasons for it;

- brainstorm solutions;

- evaluate solutions;

- give recommendations.

You should aim to focus on finding solutions rather than on attributing blame. If you concentrate on finding answers, the discussion will have a more positive attitude and be more active.

Opening statements

As discussion leader, your introduction sets the scene and should stimulate interest in all the items scheduled for discussion. Try to inject a sense of urgency so that everyone contributes. Be sure to announce the reason why you are meeting and what you hope to accomplish. Also, include some benefits for the participants: 'I want to finalise the budget for next year at this meeting. That means you will be able to plan your staffing requirements immediately and begin the year with a full production team.' Ensure that the timescale is understood, so that long, open-ended discussions are avoided.

Introduction

Give the background to the first item and open the discussion with a directed question: 'George, you're the one at the sharp end facing the public. Can you tell us what caused this latest crisis?' You could also use a general question: 'So that's the situation at present. How do the rest of you think we should tackle it?'

How to control the discussion

The most powerful method of keeping control of your group is by *asking questions* and *recapping and summarising*. I have given examples of two styles of questions (directed and general) in the section above and you can also use the following.

Redirected questions

You ask another member of the group to answer a question that has been directed to you. For example, George has stated that he will need more envelopes to complete the mailing and asks if you have any in stock. You reply, 'Mary, I think this is one for you. When will we receive the new shipment of envelopes?'

Relay question

You relay the question back to the group. 'Before I answer that let me ask *you*. Where do *you* think we should have the Christmas party?'

Reverse question

You encourage the questioner to answer his or her own question. 'What do you think? Are people prepared to pay an extra £20 for a faster service?'

Summaries

Regular summaries will help people concentrate on the main points and avoid interesting but irrelevant side issues. Previously I mentioned that in your talk or presentation you could include interest prompts and rhetorical questions to gather up the stragglers who had wandered off down Route

350. Summarising during a discussion serves a similar purpose. There are two types:

- interim summaries;
- final summary.

Interim summaries

You can report progress in the course of the discussion and help to refocus everyone's attention: 'Maybe we could leave the question of what happened at last year's Christmas party and try to decide where we want to have it this year. So far we've considered the Manor House, which is reasonably priced but difficult to get to, and the new place in the High Street, which is central but we don't know if it's any good.'

With an interim summary you can also tie up one point and move on to the next: 'So we are agreed that the people at house number 42 are letting their children run riot. The next step we need to consider, as the Residents' Association, is what we can do about it.'

Use interim summaries to highlight important points: 'We've covered the cost of the relocation and the loss of production while the factory is closed. We have also looked at the disruptive factor for our staff. Those are the main points so far.'

Don't forget the value of visually displaying the main conclusion of the meeting. You might find a flip chart useful for writing up each point as it is covered. This is visual proof that you are achieving your objectives and an encouragement to the group when the discussion appears to have become bogged down.

An important effect of summarising regularly is that it enables the minute-taker to check whether or not they have recorded the principal elements.

Final summary

Your final summing up should give a sense of achievement to the group. When a discussion has been heated, it's particularly important to draw together the various factions and unite them in a common course of action. As well as agreement from everyone, you need to establish commitment. Make sure that everyone present knows what they are responsible for and the timescale in which it must be accomplished.

SUMMARY

- Learn to love selling – it's the basis of persuasion.

- In order to be persuasive focus on your listeners' needs.

- During your discussion involve your listeners.

- Learn techniques to lead and control the discussion.

- Remember to ensure that everyone is committed and knows what they are responsible for.

20

Getting Positive Publicity from the Media

'No question is so difficult to answer as that to which the answer is obvious.'
GEORGE BERNARD SHAW

Many of the skills you have learnt in order to speak more effectively, together with your skills of persuasion, selling and conviction, also apply to media interviews. In this chapter I describe how you can benefit from any interaction with a journalist.

You may think that this chapter isn't relevant to you, as you'll never have to appear on radio or TV or even be interviewed by a newspaper journalist, but consider the value of personal publicity as well as the publicity for your organisation, or your company and its products, that is offered by any media exposure. It is free advertising: 'The business that believes that advertising is not necessary may find that customers take the same attitude about their business.' (Anon) In fact, media coverage is better than advertising. Anyone looking at an advertisement knows that it has been designed and paid for and therefore can only present a very subjective view. Your name in print or your face on TV has much more impact as people know you haven't bought the space. Presenting a positive image of your organisation in an interview is invaluable and public relations companies spend much time attempting to obtain exposure in the media for their clients and their products.

Your immediate reaction to a media approach may be to say 'no comment' or to refer the enquirer to your organisation's public relations department. This may well be the right course of action if there is a strict policy regarding talking to the media. Alternatively you may not trust the media because they seem to manipulate the truth and fail to represent accurately the views of those to whom they speak. This is a universally held view; in a recent poll journalists were rated low in integrity and honesty – in fact at about the same level as politicians! Although this is a common view of the media, it is also incorrect as far as quality papers, TV and radio are concerned, and for you to benefit from media contact, it is useful to understand how the media work.

What's the Angle?

Every story must have what is known as an 'angle'. This is the news hook or reason for its existence. When I was a radio journalist I often presented ideas for interviews or programmes to my producer, who would immediately ask me, '*Why* is this a good story? What is the point of doing it? Who is interested?' Or, more succinctly, he might say, 'So what? Who cares?' These are the questions which you must ask yourself, whether you are initiating a contact with the media or responding to an approach from them. A dull, rather humdrum subject can be of interest to the media provided you can identify a good angle. When I was seeking personal publicity a few years ago, I contacted a number of magazines before a business trip to Japan and told them that as a businesswoman in Japan, I was interested to discover whether I would be offered the male equivalent of a geisha girl. When I returned, I was interviewed by three different journalists on the problems and delights of travelling as a western businesswoman in Japan. (No, there aren't any male equivalents to geisha girls.)

The journalists' staple diet is 'News' and yet it is an indefinable term. Ask ten journalists to describe what constitutes 'News' and you will receive as many different answers. However, for the purposes of this book, I will exclude the possibility of you having to be interviewed on a major news item such as an air crash, a murder or your adulterous affair with a Hollywood star.

Coping with an Approach from the Media

You may be flattered as well as a little apprehensive when you find a journalist wants to talk to you, so here are some guidelines to help you cope.

Saying no

You can refuse to speak but be sure you understand the consequences if you choose that course of action. The journalist's first contact will be by phone and when he has described why he has approached you, you should ask for time to think about his proposal, but do return his phone call promptly as he will have deadlines to meet. On some occasions, if you decide not to speak, you can suggest an alternative person to represent your company or association. However, if your views are personal and you decline to be interviewed, you can offer to be quoted 'not for attribution'. This will enable the journalist to include your comments and maintain a balance in his story. For example, on the radio you will hear a reporter saying, 'I have spoken to several analysts within the industry and the consensus is that house prices will stabilise but there will not be a crash,' or 'Sources close to the government claim that interest rates will not be increased this week.' TV is mostly visual and 'unattributable sources', i.e. when the interviewer doesn't name his source, are quoted less frequently. On balance, I advise clients to co-operate with the media whenever possible, because your 'No comment' can easily be turned into 'They refused to speak to us' with the implication that there was something to hide.

If you have a good reason for not wanting to be interviewed, for example you don't have all the facts, or you are waiting for a report, tell the journalist why. Always refuse to comment on statements or quotations from articles by a third party until you have seen the full text. Data can be emailed rapidly across the country and around the world, so you can justifiably insist that you must read the entire quote in context before responding.

Before you say yes

When you find you have a journalist on the phone, don't be rushed into agreeing to take part in a programme or to be interviewed until you have a clear idea of what the angle is. In other words, why is the subject being covered? What makes it newsworthy? Why do they want you to contribute? Take control of the situation and of your tongue and reverse roles with the caller. Now is the time for you to interview the journalist and write down everything she says in answer to your questions. Her willingness or reluctance at this stage to discuss openly the reason for and the content of her article or programme will be a good indicator of her integrity. If necessary, ask her to slow down or repeat information until you are satisfied that you have enough data on which to base your decision to accept or decline her invitation. Find out her name, the name of her paper, or station and programme, and when and where the interview will take place (if you are going to be on a business trip in Australia on the day in question, you don't need to continue your conversation).

Here is a checklist of questions to ask before you agree to be interviewed:

- Why is the article being written or the programme being made?
- Why is the subject newsworthy?
- What is the angle?
- Why have you been approached?
- Who else's views are being sought?
- Who else will appear on the programme?
- Will it be broadcast live or will it be recorded?

If you are agreeable in principle, say so to the journalist at this point and tell her you will confirm as soon as possible. Remember that in this age of twenty-four-hour news programmes and web-based newspapers, the journalist will probably want to move quickly. With a weekly or monthly journal there may be less urgency. Whatever the deadline, give yourself time to ponder on the most important question – what's in it for you? By gaining time, you may be able to watch or listen to the programme, or read the newspaper or journal if it is not familiar to you. The Internet is wonderful for this purpose – many newspapers have on-line editions, and many radio and TV stations broadcast their programmes via the web. The BBC website in particular is a rich source of material and enables you to quickly check out the style of, say, Radio 4's *Today* programme or *You and Yours*. You will also have the opportunity to seek the views of people within your organisation as to whether you should agree to be interviewed and to decide how the organisation would benefit. Here is a checklist of questions for you to answer before you say yes:

- What's in it for me?
- What's in it for my organisation?

- Am I the best person to be interviewed?

- Do I want to be seen to associate with the other speakers or interviewees?

- Do I have sufficient time to prepare?

- Does the newspaper or journal have a good reputation?

- How am I likely to be treated by this particular journalist?

- What kind of audience or readership will this interview reach?

- Do I trust the journalist?

- What will happen if I decline the invitation?

How to Approach the Media

This is not a book about press or public relations, so I only mention a few points to bear in mind if you are the one initiating contact.

Earlier I said that the media lives on news – a term that's hard to define. However, if your contact with the media is to succeed, your story should be original and unusual, and should concern or affect sufficient people. Choosing the correct outlet for your story is important, e.g.. a new development in concrete mixers won't interest the national media, but it may be a front-page story for *Builders' Weekly*. Identify the news angle of your story, for example that the 500th employee has joined the organisation; the charity has doubled its annual collection; you have received a design award for a new product; a local councillor has returned from a fact-finding trip to China. Once you have a news hook, you must choose the correct outlet for it, for example your local newspaper or radio station may be interested in the 500th employee, particularly if you are located in an area of high unemployment; the *Design*

Gazette or local TV may be interested in the design award; and the Central Office of Information may be interested in the China trip. If you are unsure which journals or newspapers are suitable for your story, consult the media websites listed at the back of this book (see page 305). Also study the *Radio Times* and *TV Times* and listen to local radio stations.

Your initial approach to both print and broadcast media can be in the form of a press release, giving the gist of your story plus a contact name and number. Remember that during a telephone conversation with the broadcast media, they will be assessing *how* you're presenting yourself as well as the interest level of your story. Enthusiasm, vitality and sincerity are qualities that producers are always looking for. It is essential that you appear energetic, upbeat and fluent.

Try to establish a continuing relationship with your local papers and radio stations, and don't be discouraged if they don't accept your first approach, which may be due to factors outside your control, for example lack of time or space. Local TV provides limited exposure, but it is a good learning ground should you ever need to appear on national TV.

After You Have Said Yes

Preparation is the key to successful interaction with the media and planning what you want to say and what you don't want to say is the first step. Remember, you only have one chance to get it right and no one will be interested in your second thoughts.

In the same way as you drew a mind map to release all your thoughts before you wrote a word of your talk, you can do the same for your media meeting. Remember to put down all the material you don't want to reveal, as well as that which you do. Code your ideas with three colours, say red for positive ideas to include, blue for points to exclude and yellow for ideas that don't fall into either category. Your red ideas will become the kernel of your interview and from them you should develop your key statements.

Target audience

In order to prepare well, you must find out as much as possible about your audience. Who reads the newspaper? Who watches or listens to the programme? Talking to the *Financial Times* or the *Finchley Times* requires a different approach; talking to a reporter from a BBC radio news desk or from *Woman's Hour* and being interviewed by a journalist from *Newsround* (a children's TV news programme) or from BBC1's *Newsnight* are very different situations. Find out the age, sex, education and, most important, the socio-economic group of the target audience, so you can avoid talking down to the audience or losing their interest because they don't understand you.

Now is the time to familiarise yourself with the programme. Record or video it so that you can study the style and techniques used by the presenters. Is there a bias? Is there evidence of heavy editing? Read articles in the newspaper or journal and analyse how the interviews are handled. Is the story balanced? If possible, contact any other people who are to be interviewed on the same subject and arrange to speak to them beforehand. If you need more information about the programme or article contact the journalist involved. Find out some of the questions she intends to ask (she won't divulge all of them), so that you can research any additional data you might need. Put yourself in her place and that of the editor or producer and ask yourself what questions they might pose. Too often my clients find it hard to accept that difficult questions should be anticipated and the correct answers carefully worked out. Hoping against hope that the journalist won't find the skeleton in your cupboard is foolhardy. Far better to put a smart suit on your skeleton so if the cupboards do open for a moment, it won't be recognised for what it is. Plan how you can turn your negative points into positive points.

Key statements

You will have decided to be interviewed because you recognised the benefit to you or your organisation or both, and now you must identify how you want your audience to react. Remember, the journalist is not your audience. Your audience is made up of the listeners, viewers or readers. Depending on the duration of the interview, choose one or two key statements that will form the core of your answers. Don't attempt to make more than three points. Don't add too much – most successful replies are only twenty to thirty seconds long. Learn to talk in brief, colourful sentences. Find illustrations and anecdotes that will capture the imagination of your audience. Remember to avoid jargon and abbreviations that won't be understood by the general public. When dealing with the print media, you can afford to amplify your answers, but bear in mind that whatever you say will be condensed, rearranged and even cut by sub-editors after the journalist has written it.

Thorough preparation will enable you to put across your key statements concisely, colourfully and entertainingly, and will reduce the possibility of misrepresentation.

Steps in your preparation:

- research the target audience;

- identify your key statements, i.e. what you want to say and what you don't want to say;

- find colourful examples and anecdotes to illustrate your points.

- Prepare one or two simple, important statistics. Journalists love impressive numbers, for example the longest, the biggest, the smallest.

At the Radio Station

The most important factor is your voice and your ability to project *enthusiasm*, *sincerity* and *vitality*.

Radio is an informal medium and you should try to concentrate on talking to the interviewer and forget the thousands or even millions who are listening to you at home. Research shows that most radio is listened to by people on their own and there is no group identity such as you'll find in a large conference hall or in a theatre. You are not addressing a group of thousands, you are talking to a number of individuals listening to you by themselves. Your words should be simple and they should paint pictures that will stir the listeners' imaginations. Try to illustrate your key statements with colourful examples.

I heard a story on the radio recently that illustrates what I mean. It was concerning the bad behaviour of drunken passengers on holiday charter planes. A stewardess was interviewed about an occasion when a plane had to make an unscheduled landing because a passenger had become uncontrollable and was attempting to open the emergency door. In answer to a question about how the stewardess felt about these unruly passengers she said, 'It is very, very upsetting for the younger girls who have never experienced such abuse. They look forward to doing this job and when they get on the plane they find it's worse than *being a barmaid in a rough pub*.' I think in a few words she painted a very clear picture.

Don't be overawed by the studio equipment or by the interviewer. You may well be in a small overheated studio with a glass wall through which the producer and technician will be sitting. Ignore the microphone and speak in a normal voice – a technician will adjust the levels. Always ask to see the introduction to your appearance in order to check for inaccuracies. Also ask what the first question will be, so that you are prepared, but don't assume that they will actually start with the question you were expecting.

Many radio interviews are conducted over the phone: always

ensure that you are in a quiet room without interruptions and use a land-line rather than a mobile. Telephone sound quality is not as good as that of a studio so make an effort to speak clearly and with a varied upbeat style. If you feel you are 'over-performing' you have probably got it right.

Speak in a steady, conversational tone and avoid filler words ('You know', 'I mean') and refrain from beginning every answer with 'Well . . .' Don't use an impersonal style – 'People think that . . .' Instead say, 'I think that . . .' Being long-winded and rambling is a major sin. Give brief answers that don't run over thirty seconds and pause at the end of each one to enable the interviewer to ask another question. Radio interviews are generally two to three minutes in length, so you only have a short time in which to deliver your message. Avoid yes/no answers and aim to put a smile in your voice. The section on 'question time' below should help you deal with the interview.

Before you begin try to find out how long the interview will be so that you can pace your answers accordingly. Never speak over someone else, even to add your agreement – 'Mm that's right' – but raise your voice if someone is interrupting you and say, 'May I finish . . .' If the interview is recorded and you are dissatisfied with the quality of one of your answers, ask to re-record it.

If you have a tendency to fiddle, remove any temptations such as spectacles, earrings, bracelets, paper and pens. If you need a crib, write it on a card. Nerves can make you breathless, so take a couple of deep, relaxing breaths before you begin and try not to hold your breath during the interview. If the programme is recorded, make sure you know when it is scheduled for broadcast.

Television Appearances

The most memorable part of being on TV is your own appearance. Your credibility depends almost entirely on how you look, as viewers are convinced that they can instantly assess anyone within a few seconds of his appearing in their screen. In the past, politicians have often found to their cost that in spite of being proficient and experienced, they lost the support of the voters because their faces or personalities weren't popular on TV. It is unlikely that your career depends on TV success, but be aware that it is a very powerful medium.

Rehearse your body language

TV is very intimate. The TV camera comes closer to you than most of your friends. Few people look at you from a distance of only a few inches and yet a close-up on TV from your chin to your hairline reveals much of your inner feelings and thoughts. You need to build up your confidence so your uncertainty doesn't show. Remember, familiarity breeds confidence, so the more you can learn about TV before you appear, the more confident you will be. Watch the programme and notice the seating arrangements and the colour of the set; study the camera angles and become aware of the cutting from one camera to another to pick up interest points; familiarise yourself with the style of interview and the types of question that are posed.

During your practice sessions at home, try sitting in a chair similar to that which you will find in the TV studio, and avoid crossing and recrossing your legs or swinging your foot. Don't fiddle with the arm of the chair – arrange your hands calmly in your lap. Sit well back in the seat of the chair and don't slouch. While you are rehearsing in your seated position, try to put animation, enthusiasm and enjoyment into your face, but keep your head still as the camera can't keep following it if it's jerking about. If you study TV interviews and panel discussions, you'll see that most of the camera shots are of head and shoulders, so all your expression must be in your face.

Smile appropriately and maintain a confident and enthusiastic appearance, but be sure to match your look with the content of the interview. One politician I counselled had the unfortunate habit of smiling broadly when he discussed the problem of lack of childcare facilities and was unaware of the impression he created until I recorded him on video.

The point made in Chapter 11 (see page 149) about using your hands is doubly important on TV. Keep your hands away from your face, don't touch your hair, nose, mouth and don't fiddle with pens, jewellery or your clothing. Use low-key, smooth, liquid gestures as if you were underwater.

Never look at the camera – in fact, try to imagine that no one else is in the studio apart from the interviewer. When you are being introduced, look at the interviewer with interest and avoid a smug or an embarrassed grin as she lists your qualities and achievements. During questions, as well as when you are answering, keep your eyes on her and remember that the camera will often pick up your reaction to a question, so don't grimace or pull a face. In a discussion programme, look at the speaker and try to appear interested and alert; act naturally and nod or shake your head in agreement or disagreement. Remember to keep your head up because if the lighting is poor, you will appear to have heavy shadows under your eyes.

It may help you to control your nervousness to remember that the average audience for one TV set is two to three individuals, so imagine having a conversation with friends in your own sitting room and try to forget the millions who may be watching you.

What to wear on TV

Try to avoid wearing black or dark grey or even mid-blue, which comes out very dark on camera, as these colours can look too sombre, even for a business programme. Grey is most suitable for men, but avoid white shirts and choose a light colour instead. Don't wear material with any narrow stripes or checks and avoid bright red as it can 'bleed'. Also, avoid large patterns; plain colours look best on camera. Avoid jangling earrings and fussy necklines, and remember that most of the camera shots will be head and shoulders so that you should aim for a simple, plain, uncluttered look. Shiny jewellery is a distraction as it catches the light. If possible, check the colour of the background set before the programme so that you don't choose an outfit that clashes, or tones in so well that you disappear.

At the TV station

Adrenaline and alcohol don't mix so refuse a drink to calm your nerves as it may have the opposite effect. Take a deep breath instead or a small soft drink and remember to go to the toilet before and after your make-up session.

Make-up session

Modern TV lighting is less hot than in years gone by, but a studio can still be uncomfortably warm: you may well perspire and give the impression that you are under pressure and feeling uneasy. That's probably exactly how you will be feeling, but why tell millions of people? A quick pat with the powder puff will enable you to look composed. If you are fair, the lights will bleach out your colouring so expect to have your eyes made up. Allow ten minutes for the make-up session, which will be conducted by make-up experts who are also trained to calm and relax you before your appearance. If you suffer from any allergies, take your own make-up. However, don't be surprised if you are not offered make-up as many programmes don't bother these days.

In the studio

When you see the studio set for the first time, you will be surprised that it looks rather tacky and smaller than it appears on your TV at home. The person in charge in the studio is the floor manager who is in contact with the director in the production-control room, which is generally positioned above the studio behind a large glass wall. In the studio, there may be an assistant floor manager. Take the opportunity of visiting the studio before your appearance if you can, to familiarise yourself with the set-up; this will help you concentrate on the interview when it's your turn so that you can avoid being distracted while on camera.

Now it's your turn

A technician will clip on a personal mike to your shirt or jacket; it's advisable for women to wear a button-through shirt or dress as high necks without a front fastening have no suitable place to which the mike can be fixed. You should also avoid wearing silk, as this can cause crackling on the mike. Table-top and boom microphones are sometimes used as back-up and you can ignore them altogether.

When you are in position on the set, glance at the monitors on the floor in front of you to inspect your position on camera. Now is the time to straighten your tie, pull down your jacket and undo a button if necessary, or smooth your skirt and check your hair. This is not vanity – you don't want your credibility to be jeopardised by a stray wisp of hair or a crooked tie. Don't perch on the edge of the chair; sit well back so that you can easily move forwards or backwards. Try to maintain an open position towards the camera and when you make a gesture use the arm furthest from the camera.

Check your introduction with the interviewer if you have not done so already; inaccuracies and even the mispronunciation of your name in the first few seconds of the interview are not a good start. Also confirm the duration of the piece. If you are feeling tension around your mouth and eyes, do some exercises to release the stiffness, and raise and lower your shoulders to become more relaxed (see Chapter 10 for exercises to help you relax). Several deep breaths will have a calming influence. Try to ignore your thumping heart and the rest of the studio, and imagine that you are about to have a private conversation with the interviewer.

The floor manager counts down from ten to zero and the interviewer faces the camera with her introduction. From now until the end of the programme, remember that the camera may be on you at any point, even when you are not talking. When the interview is over, don't thank the interviewer and *don't move*. Stay where you are until you are told you can get up. Even though sound and lights may have faded, the cameras will probably still be on the set, so don't leap up and shout in relief that it's all over!

Question Time

Reading a newspaper article doesn't give you much insight into the questioning techniques of the journalist, but by watching and listening to television and radio interviews you can learn more about the types of question that are often used.

Open questions

As part of their everyday work, managers tend to use open questions to gain as much information as possible about a situation or a subject to help them in the decision-making process. 'So what will be the outcome if we change from cardboard to plastic containers?' 'How can we cope with the new pay demands?' 'Why did you leave your last job?' Open questions are generally prefaced with what, why, when, how, where and who. Both media and print journalists use them when they want ample and full answers to their questions. The purpose of the interview is to hear the interviewee's views and opinions, and therefore it's the journalist's job to make sure her questions prompt interesting answers.

All the media are there to inform and to entertain, and the ratio of information to entertainment varies from one programme (or newspaper) to another. *BBC News* at 10 p.m. presents a high proportion of information, but with sufficient entertainment to ensure that the viewer keeps tuned. On the other hand, a games show will have a higher degree of entertainment and less information. In any newsagents, you will notice the differing amounts of hard news or lightweight stories that dominate the front pages of the national daily newspapers. The reason I am emphasising the element of entertainment present in all media is because the journalist is aware that information alone can be dull. It is in the journalist's interest, therefore, to stimulate and provoke exciting answers from you.

Statement questions

These questions can be answered by a yes or a no response and are generally avoided by good broadcast journalists. To illustrate this point, here is an extract from an interview with the oldest man in Birmingham recorded by a local radio journalist, in which the journalist lost control by asking the wrong kind of question.

> 'I expect you're very excited to be ninety-eight years old?'
> 'No.'
> 'Well, I expect your family is very excited?'
> 'No.'
> 'I know that many people are very proud of you. Are you going to have a big party?'

'No.'

'Ninety-eight years is a grand old age and there have been many changes in Birmingham since you were born. Have you noticed a lot of changes in ninety-eight years?'

'Not really.'

'You seem very healthy for your age. What's the secret of your old age?'

'Dunno!' (He might have answered, not wasting his breath answering silly questions.)

As you can see, this doesn't make for very exciting listening. However, statement questions in the hands of a skilled *print* journalist can become a good story:

'Were you expecting such a sharp fall in the share price?'

'No!'

'I expect it came as a bit of a shock then?'

'Yes, it did!'

'What about the future? Could the price go lower?'

'Well, yes.'

This could be written as follows: 'Gold-Top Chairman, Peter Davis, is shocked by the fall in the share price, and he predicts that there is worse to come.'

How to Make Key Statements

Don't try to avoid answering the question. You have probably seen and heard politicians side-step questions and at home you find yourself saying in frustration, 'Answer the question.' Journalists are very adept at repeating and rephrasing questions, so you are ill-advised to evade them. Answer the question and, without pausing for breath, say, 'But the point I should like to emphasise is that we have had fewer accidents in our factory than any other company in this area.' This is your key statement. You can also use phrases like, 'But let me put it another way ...', followed by your key statement, or 'But what I think is really important is ...', followed by your key statement, or 'But what you shouldn't forget is ...', followed by your key statement.

Don't feel restricted by the questions but control the interview by adding your key statement. Remember to include anecdotes: 'I can best answer that question by telling you about an incident that happened in our Manchester office.'

If you are unlucky enough to be interviewed by an inexperienced journalist, you may find that he answers his own questions: 'How do you feel about winning the contract? I expect you're very pleased. Everyone at your company must be very proud, as I know the competition was very great. It certainly is a great honour.' Try not to get drawn into this verbose nonsense and ignore his prompts. 'My company, Greystone Limited, was chosen to design and build a series of hotels in Florida and California. We think it's particularly significant that a British company and one from this area was awarded the contract, as the competition from American companies was very stiff. We feel it proves that Greystone Limited represented the best in British architecture.' Don't be self-conscious about naming your product or service, as this was one of the reasons for agreeing to a media meeting and you must not lose sight of it. You may be looking at the interviewer, but you are really talking to the audience listening to you at home or who will read your comments in the newspaper. However, don't overdo the mentions of your own company or organisation; once or twice is enough and anything more may well be edited out.

Don't wait for the right question

It may appear from this that you will never win with a journalist because he will always be in control of the questions.

Remember, however, that you are in control of the answers. You have decided what you want to say and you must say it without waiting for the right question. The right question may never come or it may come at the end of a long interview and your answer may be edited out.

In the face of hostile questioning

Everyone approached by the media is concerned that they will have to defend themselves against a barrage of aggressive and abrasive questions.

Be sure you understand the difference between hard questions and hostile questions. It's the journalist's job to make an interesting programme or write an interesting article, and a cosy chat, although more comfortable for you, is dull for everyone else. The journalist represents the voice of the people, so expect him to pose the questions they would ask if put face to face with you. A reporter will often play devil's advocate to provoke a more exciting answer from you. This is an example of a bland question: 'Following your appointment as Chairman, could you describe your plans for the future of the organisation?' A better and therefore tougher question is: 'How did you formulate the new plans for the organisation' or 'How do you defend your new plans for the future of the organisation to those who say that they're not achievable?'

You shouldn't treat this as a confrontation and respond in an antagonistic manner. Never lose your cool. Simply stand your ground and defend your point of view in a reasonable tone, with facts and not emotion. If you feel you are being asked a leading question, hold up your hand and dispute it. Don't let the interviewer get away with inaccuracies or distortions of the truth.

If the journalist discovers your weak point, it is sometimes a good tactic to admit it immediately. This may well disconcert him, if he was expecting you to disagree, and it will allow you enough time during the rest of the interview to put over some positive points: 'Yes, it is true that some of our kitchens were found to be unhygienic and had to be closed, but the point I'd like to emphasise is that we have taken the opportunity to install new equipment and have decorated throughout. Everyone will be delighted that our restaurants will be reopened in time for the Christmas parties.' Don't attempt to evade questions as journalists have a highly developed sense of smell for a good story and they will keep after you, but be prepared to turn negative points into positive statements with good explanations for apparent weaknesses.

Beware of hearing more in a question than the interviewer intends. You may well have a skeleton in the cupboard that you are worried will be dragged out for all the world to see; you may even have taken the precaution of preparing some suitable answers, but listen carefully to the question. Don't fall into the trap of answering a simple question with a detailed, defensive response. Parents are often concerned with how well they will answer their children's questions about the facts of life and so the question 'Mummy, where did I come *from*?' is answered with a half-hour detailed biology lesson. The parent might be rather nonplussed when the child says, 'Thanks, Mummy, I wanted to know 'cos Darren comes from Wales.'

Sometimes you need to reveal your hand slowly, point by point. One simple piece of information may be enough to satisfy the interviewer, and if not, you still have some extra material up your sleeve. Because you have planned how you will handle problematic areas, there is no need to give the equivalent of a full-scale biology lesson immediately you hear the difficult question.

Summing up with a slant

Media journalists who are anxious to leave the listener or viewer with a particular opinion will sometimes fail to summarise accurately. If you feel that you are being misrepresented, correct the interviewer immediately in a reasonable voice. Your sincerity and honesty will make a good, lasting impression.

Off the record

Before the interview starts, you may tell the journalist that there is an area you can't answer questions about. However, if during the course of the meeting he refers to it, how should you respond? Quite simply you should remind him of your agreement: 'We did agree that you wouldn't ask questions about that because of the security aspect but I am happy to talk about the rest of the project.' Interviewers will often attempt to get you to say more than you intend, but remain calm and reasonable and refuse to answer, being sure to give the reason so that you don't appear to be concealing information. If you appear honest, sincere and straightforward you will gain credibility.

Don't repeat an interviewer's allegations in your denials: the interviewer might say, 'It appears that the company is in difficulties and close to bankruptcy.' Your reply should contain positive statements: 'That is not so. In fact, the company is on a sound financial footing and has the full backing of the shareholders.' This is a more powerful statement than: 'The company is not close to bankruptcy.'

Discussions

You'll find that the objective of a broadcast discussion is often to present a number of different points of view without necessarily reaching a specific conclusion. The choice may be left to the listener or viewer. Remember, there will be competition for airtime during the discussion and you will need to feel assertive in order to make your points.

Before you agree to take part, find out who else is on the

programme and what viewpoints they represent. The producers may seek to present a stimulating programme by having a contrast of opinions so you shouldn't expect to find fellow souls on the panel.

In order to present your opinions forcefully, you must have sufficient data to support them and to counteract arguments from your opponents. Also, remember to research into their backgrounds for further ammunition.

Discussions are often prerecorded so that the dull patches can be edited, resulting in a more enjoyable and entertaining programme. Make sure you speak in headlines and don't ramble. Listen attentively to distinguish between evidence, argument and conclusions; examine the evidence offered by the other speakers to see if it is relevant or consistent; look at the assumptions underlying their conclusions to see if they are logical and, lastly, add a touch of humour to persuade your audience.

Telephone Interviews

Print and radio interviews are very often conducted over the phone. However, if the journalist is unknown to you, try to persuade him to talk to you face to face. In this way, you are in more control of the situation and can judge how much it is advisable to say. For phone radio interviews talk in short, punchy sentences and in a normal tone of voice.

Unless you find yourself at the centre of a major news story in an inaccessible part of the world, you are unlikely to be interviewed over the phone for TV. However, interviews are occasionally conducted in a regional studio by a national interviewer in, say, London. Respond to the interviewer as if he were in the room with you and try to look animated and lively as the camera records your responses. On this occasion you do look at the camera.

Interviews in the Office

If you are fortunate enough to be offered an interview in your office, accept it. You will feel more confident when you are on home ground and it is less time-consuming for you. Make sure that the background area looks tidy and that your telephone is unplugged and your mobile silenced. Radio interviews are often conducted in offices or hotel rooms with little disruption to the normal routine, except to ban telephone calls and to switch off background noise such as air conditioning or heating. TV recordings are more disruptive, as additional people and equipment are involved, and they may need to move your furniture in order to provide a suitable background. A constant supply of tea and coffee will make you popular with everyone.

Press Conferences

These are called to respond to bad news or to announce good news.

If a negative story breaks about your company or organisation, you may want to call a press conference to refute the story or to present your own angle. Think carefully of the benefit of this because you may be in danger of prolonging a small, one-day story into a larger two-day or three-day exposure. If a press conference seems the correct path, open with a brief statement that conveys your organisation's objective. This press statement should also be in a written form, so that it can be handed out to journalists. You may choose to have two or three spokespeople present to answer questions, but ensure that a time limit is imposed from the beginning.

Good news is more fun for you but less newsworthy and so, to attract a good attendance, you must make it a special occasion. There is considerable competition for journalists' time so plan an original incentive (the 'hook' or 'peg') to draw them. The services of a good public relations company are always beneficial in all your interactions with the media, and if you find you are appearing more frequently, consider a short course in media training to build your confidence and add polish to your performance.

A Last Word

Remember to treat all journalists with respect, but not reverence or familiarity. You are the expert so listen to the question, answer it concisely and include your key statements, but challenge any misleading information.

SUMMARY

- Remember to always discover the reason for the invitation.

- Ask yourself what's in it for you.

- You will come across with more confidence if you prepare thoroughly.

- Part of your preparation should be to watch or listen to the programme or to read the newspaper.

- Prepare one or two positive, short, key messages, with one or two crisp statistics and an example or anecdote to illustrate your key point.

- Rehearse, rehearse and rehearse.

- Remain cool, calm and confident – you are the expert.

21

Handling Virtual and Cross-cultural Meetings

> 'I know that you believe you understand what you think I said, but I am not sure that you realise that what you heard is not what I meant.'
>
> ANON

Apart from handling TV, radio or the press you may find yourself giving your presentation using technology to reach an audience around the world or addressing people from different cultural backgrounds. In this chapter I examine the advantages and disadvantages of using technology to communicate and offer some suggestions on how to get the most from it; I also give a brief overview of the problems you may face with cross-cultural meetings and, lastly, provide some recommendations for using interpreters.

Virtual Meetings

Virtual meetings using audio-, data- or video-conferencing technology have increased substantially over the past few years. They not only represent significant savings in time and money, but also reduce the stress levels of managers who previously had to spend many days travelling and nights away from home.

However, there are situations and cultures where physical face-to-face communication cannot be replaced by technology. Initial meetings, where the foundation for a good working relationship is built, need to be real and not virtual. In fact, if a social element such as a meal can be introduced, this will speed up the process.

In cultures such as those of the Middle East and the Far East, business is conducted with a personal relationship focus, whereas in northern Europe and the US the focus is on striking the deal. I was unaware of this difference when I met a client from an Arab country a few years ago. I got down to business straight away, in order not to waste the valuable time of this VIP. Later I learnt that this was considered impolite and that I should have spent time on the non-business topics before indirectly raising the reason for our meeting.

In countries where the approach to time is less than precise virtual meetings may also be inappropriate. People in the Mediterranean countries and Latin America have a 'fluid' attitude to time and regard North Americans as being too inflexible. While working in the Middle East my colleagues and I were often frustrated as our client's clock seemed to run an hour behind ours.

With the virtual technologies there is a reduction in the usual channels of communication: the lack of a non-verbal expression such as a raised eyebrow or the speaker leaning forwards can affect how his message comes across during an audio conference; eye contact during a video conference may be directed towards the listeners but it will lack the impact of a speaker in the same room. Obviously nothing can replace the value of real meetings for contentious or sensitive issues, where minor nuances of body language can often say more than words.

However, even with these limitations, there is no doubt that technology plays an essential part in communication today. It is fast, immediate and ensures that the same message is received by the maximum number of people at the same time. The secret is to use the most appropriate channel for the message.

Audio-conferencing

This is suitable for a maximum of ten participants and has the benefit of being easy to set up and inexpensive. With a group of more than five participants the process will run more smoothly if a chairperson is appointed who can facilitate the management of the meeting.

The participants should introduce themselves individually at the beginning and if there are more than three or four speakers, it is helpful for the listeners if the speaker identifies himself each time before speaking. Enthusiastic participants should restrain themselves and not talk over other speakers. It's possible with an Internet link for participants to share documents and data with each other via their computers. Remember at the end of the meeting to confirm decisions, actions to be taken and deadlines to be met.

Video-conferencing

As the cost of equipment has decreased, many more organisations are using this technology for regular meetings, often within the same country. These systems can work either point to point between two sites, or multi-site via a video-conferencing service provider.

In theory any number of sites can be involved; however, four sites with three or four participants at each site is the maximum that can work effectively in practice, although you could bring in additional people on an audio line. An object or a graphics camera can highlight visual aids or even 3-D objects, and computers can add PowerPoint slides, documents and spread-sheets.

Instruction in the use of video-conferencing tends to focus on the technical detail and there is little or no training on how to present yourself to people halfway round the world. I do not intend to cover the equipment here, but simply to offer a few pointers as to what will add to or detract from the impact you make.

Before the meeting

- Identify the purpose of the meeting and what you and others are seeking to achieve. Make sure all the sites agree on this. Consider who else will be present – their needs, attitude and level of knowledge.

- Brainstorm your ideas and structure the points you need to make.

- Make a list of the key questions you may be asked and prepare answers to them. List questions you would like to ask. Decide whether you need to discuss any points with colleagues before the meeting.

- Produce an agenda and distribute it to other meeting attendees at all sites.

- Prepare notes or visuals that you will need for the meeting.

On the day of the meeting

- Tidy the room and desk and remember to keep confidential documents out of the way.

- Ensure that the television screens/camera are correctly positioned and that the camera is not facing sunlight or bright lights. Ceiling lights need to be on unless there is plenty of natural light.

- At least twenty minutes before the meeting go on-line and check and familiarise yourself with the equipment.

- Video-conferencing requires the same restrictions on clothes and accessories as appearing on TV. Therefore, try to avoid sparkling jewellery, spectacles that might catch the light, jazzy ties and clothing with plaids and narrow stripes. Also avoid large areas of white, as these can cause glare.

- When everyone is in the room check seating arrangements and enter pre-sets. If there is more than one person at each site a pre-set can include two to three people. Check the pre-sets with the other site, or sites. Each site should note the pre-sets of the other site. You can use the equipment more creatively by setting the camera pre-sets to zoom in on the speaker.

- Nominate someone to operate the control pad and someone to operate the object camera on which you can display your visuals.

- Nominate a chairperson at the master site and a meeting leader at each of the other sites. Then go through a roll call at each location so that participants can introduce themselves. Using the object camera, show your agenda to the other sites.

- You may find it useful for identification purposes to have your site name and participants' names in front of them throughout the conference.

- If you are using a voice-activated camera, two people talking simultaneously can cause rapid video switching, so ensure that the speaker at the on-screen site has finished speaking before you respond. For multi-site calls you can also put your microphone on mute and only become 'live' when you wish to speak.

- Remember, it is totally unnecessary to shout or even raise your voice above the normal conversational level.

- This is the time to practise your best pronunciation. Speak clearly and slowly. This is particularly important if you are talking to those whose mother tongue is different from yours. Be careful not to include technical shorthand or abbreviations that may be incomprehensible to other sites.

- If you are reading from notes vary your tone and pace and look up regularly towards the camera in order to maintain eye contact with the other sites.

- Your posture throughout the meeting is important; try to keep still as body, head and hand movement can cause the image to break up at the other sites. Avoid shuffling paper, coughing or carrying on side conversations that may be picked up by the microphone. Even picking up and putting down your pen or tapping a pencil will be audible and amplified.

- Be concise, avoid waffle and adding extra detail once you have finished your main point. Pause, look for the reaction and, if necessary, invite questions. Wait for a response and then continue or indicate that you are handing over to someone else.

- For private discussions with colleagues suspend the meeting for a short time. Remember to switch your microphone off, and the camera if necessary. For privacy you can also pass a note to a colleague.

Internet conferencing

You can use the Internet as an on-line meeting forum; however, it is slow and the least personal method of communicating with a group of people.

Cross-cultural Meetings

Watch your language

Many international companies use English as their corporate language and have local offices around the world. With the speed of travel and the advent of video-conferencing, at some time you will probably find yourself in a situation where your audience's mother tongue is not English.

There are a number of techniques and strategies to make sure that language differences don't affect the impact of your message. How you tackle the situation will depend on various issues:

• the size of the audience;

• how well they understand spoken English;

• the balance of mother tongue to learnt English.

Let's look at what I consider to be the easiest and probably the most common situation – a small group (under twelve people) whose mother tongue is not English, but whose knowledge is good to excellent. You don't need an interpreter, but you should be aware that you can lose your audience in a number of ways:

• Avoid double negatives: 'If we don't invest in this plant now, we won't be able to achieve targets next year.' A clearer construction would be, 'We must invest in this plant now to achieve next year's targets.'

• Be aware of double meanings to the same word. A chief executive emailed his local manager in Brazil 'fire staff with enthusiasm'. Two days later the local manager replied, 'I have followed your instruction and made 300 people redundant.'

• Avoid expressions with a national connotation, for example, collecting your P45.

- Avoid all colloquialisms: 'moving the goal-posts', 'making a pig's ear of it' or 'getting egg on your face'.

- Be aware of national sensitivities. Avoid expressions like 'He behaved like a little Hitler.'

- Avoid abbreviations and acronyms that may not travel well, for example AIDS is SIDA in French and VAT becomes TVA in French and EVA in Spanish.

With small audiences you can always invite them to say if they don't understand a particular word or expression.

Your delivery should be slower and clearer than if you were talking to people with English as their mother tongue. If you have a regional accent you may want to adopt a more received pronunciation, or think about enunciating clearly to avoid misunderstandings. The following illustrates the difficulty a foreigner may experience when listening to a native English speaker. An English manager was asked to bring along his German colleague for a discussion with a Japanese group as they could understand the German's English more easily. He was probably speaking what has come to be known as 'offshore English', with simple grammar, straightforward sentence construction and, of course, no colourful colloquialisms.

General advice on using professional language services

When seeking professional help to cope with a multilingual audience, you will meet translators and interpreters. Interpreters work with the spoken word, while translators reproduce your text in writing, working in their mother tongue.

Before making a presentation which is to be interpreted, allow sufficient time for the interpreter to check any technical terms or corporate expressions with no instant, exact translation.

In fact, some words may simply not exist. With the opening up of the Russian continent, it was discovered that no single word existed for 'marketing'. Equally, as women's equality is introduced and discussed in China, new words have to be invented in Mandarin.

It is important for the interpreter to see a transcript of your talk in advance. This avoids any such problems. Failing that, at least try to meet her before your presentation. Remember that she may have questions of her own which will help her to do a competent job for you.

Another area of difficulty is humour. I know of one speaker who was delighted with the reception that his humorous story received at a major conference. It was only later that he learnt that the interpreter had, in fact, said to the audience, 'The speaker is now telling a funny story – will you please laugh.'

Interpretation

There are various styles of interpreting. The ones you are most likely to encounter are simultaneous and consecutive.

Simultaneous interpreting

Simultaneous interpreting describes the situation where the interpreter talks at the same time as you do. This can happen in one of two ways. When the interpreter speaks quietly in the room, seated beside any member of the audience who needs assistance, this is called 'whispering interpreting'. In some situations a manager may understand the language, but be reluctant to ask a question, and would require the services of a whispering interpreter to do so on his behalf, to ensure clarity and intelligibility. If you are presenting in this situation, be aware that there will be somebody speaking in a low voice all the time during your presentation. Regular breaks should be scheduled if only one interpreter is present, as this is a tiring and intensive activity.

Alternatively, at large conferences where many people need to listen to a second language, two interpreters work in relay, seated in a soundproof booth with a large, clear window giving them full view of you and your presentation. In the latter situation, you and members of your audience need to have access to headphones in order to hear the voice of the interpreter. Anyone who speaks in the meeting room must use a microphone, which feeds sound into the booth, otherwise the interpreter cannot hear what is said.

Wherever she is seated, bear in mind that the interpreter may need longer to explain expressions and, although you may speak at a normal rate, you should plan to allow pauses between chunks of information. It is also important to avoid standing in front of a visual aid the interpreter may have to refer to or even translate. In an ideal layout, you should be in visual contact with the interpreter. Any verbal communication would normally be made through the chairperson of the meeting.

If you are to use a microphone to speak or headsets in order to listen to interpreters during a question-and-answer session, it is always advisable to check the settings and ask technicians for advice on how to use them before making your presentation.

Consecutive interpreting

When the interpreter waits until you have finished speaking before repeating what you have said in the other language, this is called 'consecutive interpreting'.

The same issues need to be considered as for simultaneous interpreting. However, in this situation, after expressing each chunk of ideas you will need to wait for the interpreter to finish repeating this, before continuing with your presentation. Again, it is important for the interpreter to have a copy of your script in advance so that any difficulties may be identified and resolved.

Don't forget that if, for any reason, the interpreter is prevented from understanding or following your presentation, you will lose the opportunity to get your message across to part of your audience.

Visual aids

If you are presenting to an international audience you must decide the language of your visual aids. The IT company Cisco Systems uses English visual aids, even when presenting in a foreign language. Often the terms are extremely technical and no translation exists. If you face this situation, it is important to explain the terms and possibly add another visual aid for greater clarity. Although I stressed my dislike of word slides in Chapter 6 (see page 82), when presenting to an international audience I feel they can help to put your message across.

This is particularly true when addressing Japanese audiences who, in general, have a greater command of written English than spoken English. During a meeting in Tokyo a Japanese manager presented me with a sheet of bullet points. He went on to explain each one; however, I was grateful for his notes as his accent was strong which made it difficult to understand him. He was obviously aware of this and had overcome the problem with his bullet point sheet.

If you are responsible for organising a conference or meeting, it is essential that you advise delegates that an interpretation service will be available. This will encourage attendance by anyone who may doubt their ability to follow or contribute to proceedings in the main language of the meeting.

Final Words

If in doubt, tackle the problem head-on, as one speaker did when addressing a bilingual conference. 'It's common for the English to start their presentation with a joke. I am French, but I am speaking in English, so what should I do?' This was, I think, a very acceptable way of building a rapport with both the English and the French members of the audience.

SUMMARY

- Be aware of the limitations of virtual meetings.

- Choose the most appropriate channel for the successful outcome of your communication.

- Consider engaging a professional language services company, if necessary, for multi-cultural meetings.

22

And Finally . . .

As I write the last few pages of this book, it makes me think of how you might feel the day after a particularly important speech. For weeks, maybe even months, it has been on your mind – sometimes in the forefront as you grappled with the right choice of words; sometimes in the background as you watched a television programme and realised that you could use an amusing line from a comedy show. Then suddenly it's over. It took months to prepare and only moments to deliver. You might think you are like a runner who prepares for a 100m sprint at the Olympic Games. In fact, speaking is not like that at all. There is no winner in the speaking game. Rarely is speaking a one-off event. Developing your ability to speak effectively is a continuous process.

Now you've read this book, you will see its basic difficulty: that you can't learn to speak just by reading. Trying to do so would be like trying to learn to ride a bike from a book. I've written about the techniques but that is only a tiny fraction of effective speaking. Now you are able to identify all the parts of the bike, you understand the principles of balance and where you should put your hands and feet. You know how to indicate where you're going. Now is the moment to hop on and have a ride.

Reading this book or any other won't make you a good speaker, but practising will. Unfortunately, unlike bike riding, you can't use a quiet back street to learn the basics of speaking. You need an audience to judge its effectiveness. They will be there to see all your attempts to keep your balance and to witness the occasional crash. But crashes are part of the learning process. If you've ever watched a baby learning to walk you'll know that initial failures are inevitable. The trick is not to be discouraged. Imagine a baby saying to itself as it fell back on its bottom for the umpteenth time, 'I'll never get the hang of this. I'm just making a fool of myself, I'll have to give up.' You must keep at it.

Opportunities to Practise

Learning to ride a bike with stabilisers makes it easier and you can do a similar thing with speaking in public. If you feel shy, search out low-risk occasions where you can speak, for example to the sixth form at your old school, or at the local sports club. If you are totally inexperienced set yourself the goal of asking a question at your next meeting. I know speakers who attend public meetings with the sole objective of asking a question. They sit close to the front so that they can't be ignored. As soon as question time is announced, up shoot their hands to 'speak in public'. If you decide to practise like this you will probably find you experience the same symptoms of nervousness as you do when you are giving a talk. Your heart will beat faster and you'll have a dry mouth and sweaty palms. Acknowledge all your feelings; don't try to fight them. Be aware of your physical state, but don't allow it to control you.

There are a number of speaking clubs whose sole purpose is to help members improve their speaking skills. As everybody is in the same boat a supportive environment is created which enables everyone to develop their potential. You will find website details of such clubs under Useful Websites (see page 305).

Always look for opportunities to practise. If you are attending a meeting where you have not been given a specific role, ensure that you speak up within the first ten minutes. The longer you leave it the more difficult it will be to contribute. Simply offer agreement, 'Yes that's true, we've noticed that too' or ask for more information, 'Could you give me an example of how that happened?' Speaking up early will establish your presence and make it easier for you to speak again.

As you become more proficient, consider volunteering to chair a meeting or to give a vote of thanks at your social club. Each occasion will be a challenge and an opportunity to become familiar with your anxiety. Turn it into positive energy to stimulate original thoughts and entertaining ideas.

Enjoyment

If you are an experienced speaker you probably know already how you could become more effective. Maybe there is only one reason why this doesn't happen: lack of time. You know that you should pay more attention to your preparation. You realise you should rehearse. You understand the value of good visual aids but you don't have the time. No one can change that but you. The presentations and talks you give may not be crucial to you, but if you want to improve as a speaker you'll need to make the time for it. Going on courses or reading books won't change you from being a mediocre speaker into an exceptional one. Only you can do that.

Effective speakers find time to prepare and practise, but the most vital part of a good speaker is much more difficult to acquire. It's in their hearts and shines out for everyone to appreciate. It's the magical quality of enjoyment. In other chapters I have stressed enthusiasm, sincerity and vitality. These are all based on the speaker's ability to enjoy communicating with his or her audience. Enjoyment is contagious. The audience will enjoy your talk if you enjoy giving it.

Thank you for being a good listener. I suspect you haven't agreed with everything I've said, but I hope that my suggestions will help you to capture the butterflies and train them to fly in formation.

Further Reading

Atkinson, Max, *Lend Me Your Ears: All You Need to Know About Making Speeches and Presentations*, Vermilion, 2004

Bowden, John, *Making the Father of the Bride's Speech: Etiquette; Jokes; Sample Speeches; One-liners*, How To Books, 2004

Calvert, Philip, *Make a Great Wedding Speech*, How To Books, 2005

confetti.co.uk, *The Best Man's Speech: A Tough Job Made Easy*, Conran Octopus, 2004

confetti.co.uk, *Jokes, Toasts and One-Liners for Wedding Speeches: Original Lines to Make Them Laugh and Cry*, Conran Octopus, 2004

Cooper, Anne, *Off the Cuff: What to Say at a Moment's Notice*, Career Press, 2004

Copestake, Stephen, *Powerpoint 2003 in Easy Steps*, Computer Stop, 2004

Davies, Philippa, *Total Confidence*, Piatkus, 2001

Dickson, Anne, *Difficult Conversations*, Piatkus, 2004

Glass, Lillian, *Confident Conversation: How to Talk in Any Business or Social Situation*, Piatkus, 1991

Herman, Jeff and Herman, Deborah, *Toasts for All Occasions*, Career Press, 1998

Hughes, Dominic and Phillips, Benedict, *The Oxford Union Guide to Speaking in Public*, Virgin Books, 2004

Leeds, Dorothy, *Secrets of Successful Interviews: Tactics and Strategies for Winning the Job You Really Want*, Piatkus, 1993

Pittenger, William, *Toasts and Forms of Public Address for Those Who Wish to Say the Right Thing in the Right Way*, Indypublish.com, 2003

PowerPoint 2003 Step by Step – Online Training, Microsoft Press International, 2003

Rodenburg, Patsy, *The Right to Speak: Working with the Voice*, Methuen Publishing Ltd, 1992

Safire, William (ed.), *Lend Me Your Ears: Great Speeches in History*, W.W. Norton & Company Ltd, 2004

Useful Websites

www.presentations.com
American site with valuable tips and techniques for business presenters.

www.abc.planet-typography.com
Gives details of different fonts to help you choose the most appropriate ones for your visual aids.

www.clearlypresented.com
A company specialising in designing good PowerPoint slides for presentations.

www.infoplease.com
Thousands of useful and interesting facts about every imaginable subject.

www.thesaurus.com
Language, words and puzzles.

www.quotationspage.com
21,000 quotations on-line from over 2,500 authors.

www.aphids.com/quotes
Quotation site which you can access by subject; also has a special-interest section of quotations about love and marriage which are often useful for people who need to make a toast at a wedding.

www.jokes.com
An American site which rates the jokes as Squeaky Clean, Tame or Racy.

www.office-humour.co.uk
Cartoons, one-liners and video clips.

www.toastmasters.org
An organisation with local clubs all over the world. Click on 'find a club' on the website to locate your nearest club.

www.the-asc.org.uk
Website for the Association of Speakers Clubs with 150 speaking clubs; claims to be the largest organisation within the UK promoting the skills of public speaking.

www.nsaspeaker.org
National Speakers' Association – club for those who wish to use their speaking skills professionally.

www.willingspressguide.com
Willings Guide to websites.

www.pims.co.uk
Pims (UK) Ltd offers a range of services, from digital and litho printing, direct marketing and fulfilment services, to news-release distribution and contact databases.

Index